THE NEW MORALITY

A PROFILE OF AMERICAN YOUTH IN THE 70's

DANIEL YANKELOVICH

McGraw-Hill Book Company

New York • St. Louis • San Francisco • London • Düsseldorf
Kuala Lumpur • Mexico • Montreal • Panama • São Paulo
Sydney • Toronto • Johannesburg • New Delhi • Singapore

The study on which this book is based was jointly funded by the Edna McConnel Clark Foundation, the Carnegie Corporation of New York, the Hazen Foundation, the JDR 3rd Fund, and the Andrew W. Mellon Foundation.

123456789MUMU7987654

Library of Congress Cataloging in Publication Data

Yankelovich, Daniel.
    The new morality.

    1.   Youth—United States.   2.   United States—
Social conditions—1960-   —Public opinion.
3.   College students—United States—Attitudes.
I.   Title.
HQ796.Y274   301.43'15'0973   74-11100
ISBN 0-07-072241-2
ISBN 0-07-072240-4 (Pbk.)

CONTENTS

INTRODUCTION

This study is the fifth in a series of research projects on American youth carried out by Daniel Yankelovich, Inc., since 1967. In breadth and scope of findings, it is, by far, the most ambitious of the studies done to date. Previous research (with one exception) concentrated on college youth. While the present study also concerns itself with college youth, it includes high school students, blue-collar workers, housewives, minority groups, high school dropouts, Vietnam veterans, and all the other heterogeneous groups that make up the full variety of America's youth population, age sixteen to twenty-five.

Perhaps even more important than increased breadth of coverage is the added dimension of trend measurement. This series of youth studies reflects social change in an era crowded with events that have deeply affected the lives of young people. The period from 1967 to 1973, though not long by historical standards, stretches from the peak of the Vietnam War protest movement to the disappearance of the war as an issue among young people. It is also the period in which the Women's Movement has sought to raise the consciousness of the nation, especially among young people. In this same period we have seen sweeping changes in sexual morality, work-related values, a changing climate of mistrust of our basic institutions, and other challenges to traditional beliefs and values. These events—some are universal in scope, while others affect only small portions of the population—give us an opportunity to assess the impact of social change on what is probably our most change-sensitive population group—America's young people.

Measuring changes in the national psychology by survey methods is comparatively new. From the 1930s on, we have had political polls and surveys to inform us about the country's attitudes toward political issues and candidates. But there have been few studies, national in scope, that measure changes in people's values, aspirations, beliefs, expectations, and outlook. Because the approach is new, its strengths and limitations are not yet clear. The survey method has the incomparable virtue of permitting researchers to gather information about large populations by interviewing a comparatively small handful of people—provided that cross sections are scientifically selected.

On the other hand, survey findings are difficult to interpret. What people say they believe is an imperfect guide to what they really mean and how they behave. And yet, when the pattern of inquiry in a survey has been carefully guided by previous research and by the wealth of theory that exists today in the behavioral sciences, it can throw much light on phenomena of great interest and importance.

Because interpreting the survey data inevitably involves subjective judgments, we have sharply separated the interpretive and descriptive parts of this report. The report is divided into three major sections, an overview section that interprets what we believe the findings mean, and two findings sections that present the research in a straightforward, reportorial, and descriptive fashion. In the interest of brevity, we have kept the interpretive section short and selective, focusing on what we regard as the major themes illuminated by the research. Even the descriptive sections are comparatively short in order to serve as a summary of the highlights of the research. A Research Report in five volumes that presents the data in a more comprehensive tabular form is available for loan from any of the sponsoring foundations. We describe below some of the principal characteristics of the survey.

The sample is based on 3,522 one- to two-hour personal interviews with a cross section of the country's youth population, age sixteen to twenty-five. Because a large proportion of the people in this age bracket are currently attending college, we derived the national youth cross section from two independent samples. The first sample covered the college campus population and was drawn from a representative selection of the country's two-year and four-year colleges and universities. A total of 1,006 college students were interviewed.

The second sample, in which 2,516 young people were interviewed, was based on a national probability sample of all households in the country with household members between the ages of sixteen and twenty-five. To avoid duplication with the college sample, all young people between the ages of sixteen and twenty-five living at home but attending college were eliminated from this sample. The results are projectable to the population covered. (Copies of the questionnaire and a technical appendix are available from the organizations that sponsored the study.) All interviewing on the study was conducted in the late Spring of 1973.

The earlier studies used as a basis for comparing trends include:

A 1967 study for *Fortune* Magazine, reported in January, 1968.[1]

A 1969 study for CBS News, *Generations Apart.*[2]

A 1971 report for the JDR 3rd Fund and the Task Force on Youth, *Youth and the Establishment.*[3]

A 1971 survey for the JDR 3rd Fund, *The Changing Values on Campus.*[4]

To take full advantage of the previous studies in tracking trends, the current study includes many of the same questions asked in the earlier studies, and, for the most part, the earlier sample designs were replicated. In addition to the comparative questions, the current study adds a host of new questions to examine new issues and values.

In analyzing the findings, we have used three principal measurements.

1. **Trend Data.**   Our bench mark for tracking the changes in the values and attitudes of the noncollege majority of young people is the 1969 study *Generations Apart,* which was conducted for CBS News in connection with three television programs about American youth. The 1969 study, like the present one, included samples of both college and noncollege youth. Since each one of the four earlier studies included a representative cross section of college students, we are fortunate in having a larger number of readings on changing values on campus.

---

[1]"A Special Kind of Rebellion," *Fortune* Magazine, New York, January, 1969.

[2]*Generations Apart*, Columbia Broadcasting System, Inc., 1969.

[3]*Youth and the Establishment*, JDR 3rd Fund, Inc., New York, February, 1971.

[4]*The Changing Values on Campus,* Washington Square Press, New York, 1973.

2. **The Comparison of College and Noncollege Views.** A dramatic measure of differences in values and outlook is made possible by comparing the responses of college and noncollege youth to the same questions. On some issues, college and noncollege youth react alike; on most issues, their views are different, reflecting social class and income differences, the impact of the college culture, and the sharply varied situations of the two groups. (Many of the young people not attending college are married and settled with jobs and children.)

3. **Special Group Profiles.** We have also looked at some major subgroups in the youth population separately, including:

Blue-collar workers and their work outlook and interests.

Minority youth and how they are similar to and different from their age peers.

Young people currently attending high school.

College graduates who have joined the work force.

Students attending college who are career-oriented, in contrast to those whose motives for going to college are more vague, diffuse, and intangible.

Vietnam Veterans.

The unemployed, compared to those who are working or still in school.

College and noncollege women.

In addition, the tabular Research Report, available on loan from the sponsoring organizations, presents a wealth of information about many of the other sectors who comprise today's youth generation, including young union members, housewives, high school dropouts, etc. Data are available, too, by standard demographic variables such as age, sex, type of education, background, religion, and political orientation.

This study was sponsored by the JDR 3rd Fund, Carnegie Corporation of New York, Edna McConnel Clark Foundation, Hazen Foundation, and Andrew W. Mellon Foundation.

We are grateful for the generous support that enabled us to carry out what we hope will be a useful contribution to the country's understanding of the views, values, and perspectives of American youth in a time of ferment.

Daniel Yankelovich, President
Ruth Clark, Senior Vice President
Daniel Yankelovich, Inc.

ONE
OVERVIEW

TURNABOUT

These first few years of the decade of the 1970s point to vast changes in the complexion and outlook of an entire generation of young people. Indeed, so startling are the shifts in values and beliefs between the late 1960s, when our youth studies were first launched, and the present time that social historians of the future should have little difficulty in identifying the end of one era and the beginning of a new one. Rarely has a transition between one decade and the next seemed so abrupt and so full of discontinuities. Listed below, in schematic form, are almost twenty large-scale changes revealed by the research as having occurred between the late 1960s and the early 1970s.

Late 1960s	Early 1970s
The campus rebellion is in full flower.	The campus rebellion is moribund.
New life styles and radical politics appear together: granny glasses, crunchy granola, commune-living, pot smoking, and long hair seem inseparable from radical politics, sit-ins, student strikes, protest marches, draft card burnings.	An almost total divorce takes place between radical politics and new life styles.
A central theme on campus: the search for self-fulfillment *in place of* a conventional career.	A central theme on campus: how to find self-fulfillment *within* a conventional career.

3

Late 1960s	Early 1970s
Growing criticism of America as a "sick society."	Lessening criticism of America as a "sick society."
The Women's Movement has virtually no impact on youth values and attitudes.	Wide and deep penetration of Women's Liberation precepts is underway.
Violence on campus is condoned and romanticized; there are many acts of violence.	Violence-free campuses; the use of violence, even to achieve worthwhile objectives, is rejected.
The value of education is severely questioned.	The value of education is strongly endorsed.
A widening "generation gap" appears in values, morals, and outlook, dividing young people (especially college youth) from their parents.	The younger generation and older mainstream America move closer together in values, morals, and outlook.*
A sharp split in social and moral values is found within the youth generation, between college students and the noncollege majority. The gap *within* the generation proves to be larger and more severe than the gap *between* the generations.	The gap within the generation narrows. Noncollege youth has virtually caught up with college students in adopting the new social and moral norms.
A new code of sexual morality, centering on greater acceptance of casual premarital sex, abortions, homosexuality, and extramarital relations is confined to a minority of college students.	The new sexual morality spreads both to mainstream college youth and also to mainstream working-class youth.
The challenge to the traditional work ethic is confined to the campus.	The work ethic appears strengthened on campus but is growing weaker among noncollege youth.
Harsh criticisms of major institutions, such as political parties, big business, the military, etc., are almost wholly confined to college students.	Criticism of some major institutions are tempered on campus but are taken up by the working class youth.
The universities and the military are major targets of criticism.	Criticism of the universities and the military decrease sharply.
The campus is the main locus of youthful discontent; noncollege youth is quiescent.	Campuses are quiescent, but many signs of latent discontent and dissatisfaction appear among working-class youth.
Much youthful energy and idealism is devoted to concern with minorities.	Concern for minorities lessens.

---

*Based, in part, on Yankelovich Surveys among cross sections of the general population.

Late 1960s	Early 1970s
The political center of gravity of college youth: left/liberal.	No clear-cut political center of gravity: pressures in both directions, left and right.
The New Left is a force on campus: there are growing numbers of radical students.	The New Left is a negligible factor on campus: the number of radical students declines sharply.
Concepts of law and order are anathema to college students.	College students show greater acceptance of law and order requirements.
The student mood is angry, embittered, and bewildered by public hostility.	There are few signs of anger or bitterness and little overt concern with public attitudes toward students.

Changes of this magnitude in so brief a time span are rare, at least within behavioral science experience. Also, the many reversals of directions and shifts in values seem so uncharacteristic of the normal orderly processes of human change that one is obliged to look beneath the surface for underlying causes. Our analysis leads us to conclude that this extraordinary pattern of change has been caused by two unrelated factors.

The first is the Vietnam War. The war hit young people with great force, especially on the nation's campuses. It evoked strong passions and extreme forms of behavior that reached their peak at the time of the 1970 research, conducted shortly after the Cambodia and Kent State episodes. The findings of the current research indicate that with the termination of the war and the draft that accompanied it, youthful attitudes and values have now reverted to more familiar patterns. The war, then, is one of the keys that unlocks the mystery of the dramatic pattern of changes detected by the research over these past few years.

The other force that underlies these large scale changes is more subtle but also more important because it points toward the future rather than the past. The findings of the current study show in great detail the effects of the diffusion of a set of new values that incubated on the nation's campuses in the 1960s and have now spread out to the entire youth generation. The New Values (as we shall refer to them) cover a broad range of beliefs. It may be useful here to spell out what we mean by the New Values. We use the term as shorthand for three categories of value change.

The first category refers to new moral norms—beliefs that guide the behavior of people on matters of individual and public morality. The major value changes under this heading are (1) changes in sexual morality in the direction of more liberal sexual mores; (2) changes relating to the authority of institutions, such as the authority of the law, the police, the government, the boss in a work situation, etc., in the direction of what sociologists call "deauthorization," i.e., a lessening of automatic obedience to, and respect for, established authority; (3) changes in relation to the church and organized religion as a source of guidance for moral behavior; and (4) changes associated with traditional concepts of patriotism and automatic allegiance to the idea of "my country right or wrong."

The second category of New Values relates to social values, primarily to changing attitudes toward the work ethic, marriage and family, and the role and importance of money in defining the meaning of success.

The third category of New Values concerns the meaning of the vague concept of self-fulfillment. Self-fulfillment is usually defined by people today in opposition to concern with economic security. At issue is the individual's feeling that there must be more to life than a slavish devotion to keeping one's nose to the grindstone. Once a person feels that he can take some degree of economic security for granted, he begins to look forward to relief from the discipline of a constant preoccupation with economic security, and he starts to search for forms of self-fulfillment that go beyond the daily routine. Stress on the theme of self-fulfillment is the individual's way of saying that there must be something more to life than making a living, struggling to make ends meet, and caring for others. The self-fulfillment concept also implies a greater preoccupation with self at the expense of sacrificing one's self for family, employer, and community.

Schematically, then, the New Values have three sets of interrelated meanings:

Set 1. **Moral Norms** deal with sex, authority, religion, and obligations to others.

Set 2. **Social Values** deal with money, work, family, and marriage.

Set 3. **Self-Fulfillment** is defined in opposition to role obligations to others and to the nose-to-the-grindstone quest for economic security.

As the New Values spread from a small minority of privileged college students to the mainstream of college youth, and from college youth to the noncollege majority of young workers, housewives, high school students, etc., they evoked new questions and posed new dilemmas for each of the various subgroups in the population. When people's expectations are raised and their values transformed, they seek out new patterns of fulfillment, depending on their circumstances. The well-educated and well-trained college graduate, for example, finds himself in a better position to gratify his new desires than someone who is less well trained, less well educated and privileged, even though both persons may share similar desires. If there are any patterns which underlie the dense variety of findings described in the main body of this report, they are the story of the transmission of the New Values from the campus to the mainstream of American youth, the efforts of both college and noncollege youth to find a satisfactory means of blending the New Values with older, more traditional beliefs, and the search for new modes of adaption to the highly institutionalized structure of American society.

In the material that follows, we first describe the effects of the two forces that have transformed the outlook of American youth—the end of the Vietnam War and the transmission of the New Values from a campus minority to the youth population overall. We then examine the implications of these changes (a) for college and noncollege youth and (b) for their impact on youth's opinion of the substantive issues relating to work and career, politics, and the role of women.

THE VIETNAM WAR

Some of the changes depicted in this study, such as the renewed quiet on campus and the new seriousness of students in their pursuit of careers, may appear, at first glance, to reinforce the widely held view that the 1960s represented an odd aberration in our national history. The 1970s, it is said, have restored "normalcy," linking up in a chain of continuity with the 1950s and other more familiar periods in our national history. These observers point to the striking parallelism between the "privatism" of the 1950s when young people were preoccupied with their own personal lives and destinies, and the privatism of the 1970s with its similarly strong focus on self.

The findings of the present study suggest that this conclusion is a half-truth; that is, it is partly true and partly false. The 1960s *were* characterized by many unique events which may have momentarily sidetracked the slow, steady continuity of American social history. The short but vivid era of the Kennedy presidency, the rise of the Civil Rights Movement under the leadership of Martin Luther King, the abrupt impact of the inner city riots and burnings swiftly followed by the student riots on campus, the shock of the assassinations of John and Robert Kennedy and Martin Luther King—all these events—certainly left their mark on the times.

The one event which these findings suggest most strongly influenced the values and views of a generation was, of course, the Vietnam War. It is possible to see now, in retrospect, that the spurt of political radicalism on campus was inextricably interrelated with student response to the war in Southeast Asia. The war and the draft forged an intensely personal link between the students and a far-off war which inspired loathing, fear, and revulsion on campus. The small core of political radicals, though never more than 10-15 percent of the college population, took the lead in interpreting the war in terms that were harshly critical of the United States, its motives, its institutions, and its moral impulses. Because they were so disturbed by the war, the great mass of college students accepted the radical critique and, especially in the Ivy League colleges, joined with the New Left in its attack on universities and other institutions that were interpreted as being part of the web of immorality and misuse of power that students associated with the war. Inevitably, the Vietnam-inspired political radicalism became entangled with the cluster of new life styles and social values that had their genesis in an earlier period.

Once the war passed and the draft ended, the situation changed dramatically. Describing the findings of the 1971 study, we concluded: "Radical political values and life style values which traveled together since the mid-1960s have, in 1971, begun to go their separate ways. Changing cultural values—relationships to marriage, authority, religion, work, money, career, sexual morality, and other aspects of the puritan ethic—have become more marked and dramatic each year since these measurements began, including 1971, while political beliefs have moved to the opposite direction away from their 1970 peaks. . . . The vast majority of students—the 89 percent who do not identify with the New Left—have pressed forward in their search for a cultural revolution while taking a step backwards from political revolution."[1]

Now, several years later, this same conclusion is further reinforced by the new study. The recent findings imply that it was the Vietnam War, more than any other single factor, that inspired the wave of political radicalism on campus. Although the war has left a residue of feelings which we will comment on later, it now seems reasonable to conclude that the 1960s were an aberration and a departure from the mainstream of American social history to the extent that these youthful values were so intimately tied to the war and the strong emotions it evoked, they came and went with the war.

Does this mean that we are back to the *status quo ante*? Does it imply that we are now picking up the threads of cultural continuity from where they left off in the 1950s, without the 1960s leaving any enduring mark on the present period? The findings of the present study show clearly and vividly

[1]*Changing Values on Campus*, p. 7.

that nothing could be further from the truth. Apart from the impact of the war, the 1960s were not an aberration, but an inherent part of our cultural continuity. The war was like having a despised stranger living in your home at the same time that a baby was born to the family. With the departure of the stranger, the situation may at first seem to return to what it was earlier, but it soon becomes apparent that the new baby has created its own pattern of changes in the life of the family. The war was vivid and traumatic while it lasted, but the enduring heritage of the 1960s is the new social values that grew on the nation's campuses during that same fateful period and now have grown stronger and more powerful.

THE NEW VALUES

The central theme of the present study is the story of how various subgroups in the current generation of youth are now seeking to make an accommodation to the New Values. Perhaps the most lucid way to interpret the dense wealth of findings of this study is to regard them as a case history of "cultural diffusion." Social science has made us familiar with the process. Social change is often initiated by small extremist groups. The mass of the public react initially by rejecting the new ideas, and then begin to consider them with tempered selectivity. The proposals of the extremist groups become, in effect, a vast smorgasbord from which people of more moderate temperament pick and choose those ideas that fit best with their own traditional life styles. The process may be maddening to the purists, but a remarkable amount of social change is eventually effected.

In the mid-1960s we identified a subgroup of college students as "Forerunners." This group—never a majority of the college population—struggled to live by a new set of post-affluent values. We were struck by two motivations that seemed to enjoy exceptional strength among the so-called Forerunner students: one was private, directed toward personal self-fulfillment; the other was public, directed toward a vision of what a just and harmonious society might be.

In their struggle to live by the New Values and to establish new institutions more responsive to their needs, students holding the New Values had an unfortunate tendency to demean the old values (due, in part, to an inherent youthful tendency toward moral absolutism). The New Values, therefore, surfaced on the American scene in the form of a *counter*culture. In the early 1960s, when these values first began to appear, the students who were experimenting with them, for the most part, reacted against and counter to pre-vailing traditions. As Kenneth Keniston observed, they represented an antithesis to traditional values, not a synthesis of what is valid in both the old and the new. In the experimental years of the 1960s, the college-student minority attacked virtually every belief and value cherished by the American public.

They rejected economic well-being as an indispensable source of the freedom and dignity of the individual. They derided society's definition of education as the royal road to success and achievement. They belittled the efforts of the average person to cope with the economic harshness of every-day life and his struggle to stand on his own two feet and retain some measure of autonomy within the complex conditions of modern life. They professed beliefs that seemed to flout faith in marriage, work, family, patriot-ism, democracy, competition, and equality of opportunity. They downgraded traditional American aspirations for more material comfort—more money, more education, more leisure, and more opportunities for one's self and one's children. They challenged established authority in the larger society in every one of its forms—the law, the police, the universities, the elected officials, the professions, the corporate structure, etc. They countered the traditional social institutions of marriage and church with new styles of communal living and new forms of religious expression. They scrutinized each element of traditional sexual morality for opportunities to try something different. They countered the alcohol culture with the drug culture. They met the old empha-sis on private careers with a new craving for community—the list could be continued indefinitely.

Much of the public hostility to the college movement of the 1960s was evoked by this compulsive opposition to traditional beliefs, as well as by the alien political views of the college minority. Describing the emergence of the New Values in the 1970s, we noted: "Small groups of students take extreme positions on the new values, larger groups take more moderate positions. Gradually, many of the new values will work their way from the Forerunner college group to the career-minded majority of college students and then to other young people, and then to upper-middle-class older people in urban settings, and then to the mass of the populations. At each stage in the proc-ess, a synthesis of the old and new will finally be reached although the process may take decades and perhaps generations to complete and may become sidetracked."[2] Our prediction that the process of diffusion might

---

[2]*Youth and the Establishment*, p. 84.

take decades and even generations to accomplish has been proven incorrect by the present study. Indeed, we are amazed by the rapidity with which this process is now taking place, by its complexity, and by the problems of adaption it poses to the institutions of the society. The balance of this chapter describes the effects of this wider diffusion of the New Values on and off campus.

2
CROSS-PURPOSES ON CAMPUS

ASSIMILATING THE NEW VALUES

Since Chapter 6 of this report, *The Campus as Pacesetter*, presents a detailed picture of campus trends, we will confine our commentary in this section to a few basic points.

The campus situation can be summed up as follows: the New Values are now widely diffused throughout the total college population and are no longer confined to a minority. In some categories (e.g., sexual morality) the spread continues unabated. In other categories (e.g., attitudes toward work) there has been a moderate reversal of earlier trends. The overall picture is one of a steady process of dispersion and assimilation of the New Values. The charts that follow provide some illustrations of the changes.

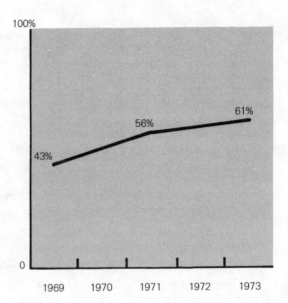

**Would Welcome
More Acceptance
of Sexual Freedom
(College Youth)**

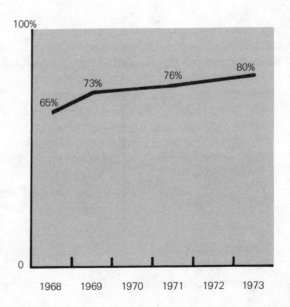

**Would Welcome
Less Emphasis
on Money
(College Youth)**

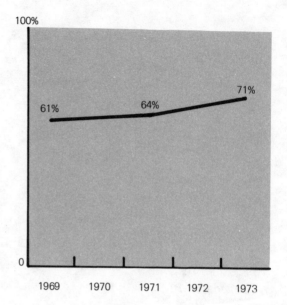

**Privacy as a Very
Important Value
(College Youth)**

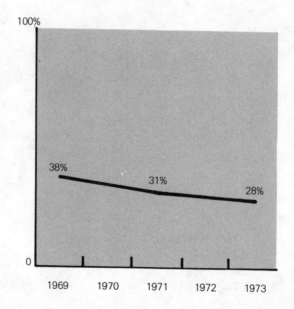

**Religion as a Very
Important Value
(College Youth)**

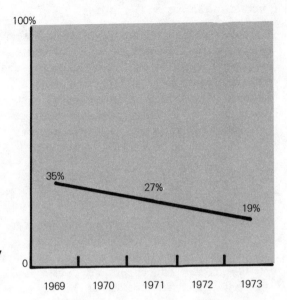

Patriotism as a Very Important Value (College Youth)

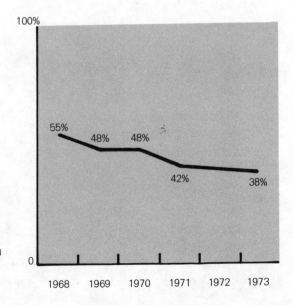

Prohibition Against Marijuana Easily Accepted (College Youth)

Career Aspirations on Campus

At the same time that the New Values have spread, there has also been a steady increase in traditional career aspirations on campus, such as the desire to get ahead, to find economic security, and to enjoy careers which provide opportunities for both money and greater self-expression and self-fulfillment. The size of the career-minded group of college students, i.e., those young people whose major purpose in going to college is to train themselves for a career, has steadily grown over the past six years. These points are illustrated in the series of charts that begins at the bottom of this page.

The Dilemma

What we see, therefore, is the simultaneous growth of two sets of values that are in conflict with each other at many points. For example, the de-emphasis on money grubbing is a cardinal tenet of the New Values. At the same time, however, the opportunity to earn good money is one of the key attractions of a conventional career. The tension created by these two conflicting value systems defines the central problem, or dilemma, that presents itself to today's college youth. Since our college population is large and

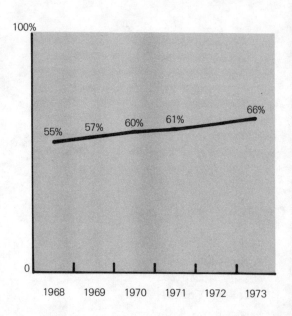

Size of the "Career-Minded" Group (College Youth)

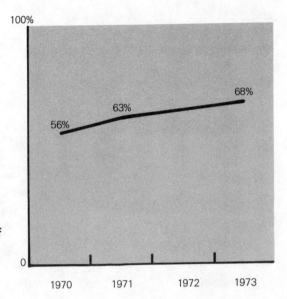

**Ability
to Express Yourself
as a Very
Important Value
(College Youth)**

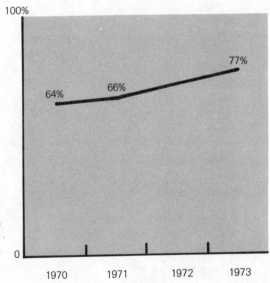

**Challenge of the Job
as an Important
Criterion
(College Youth)**

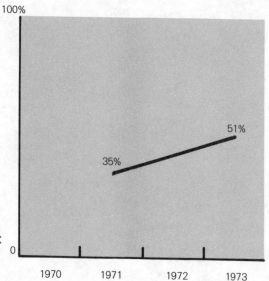

**Chance to Get
Ahead as an Important
Job Criterion
(College Youth)**

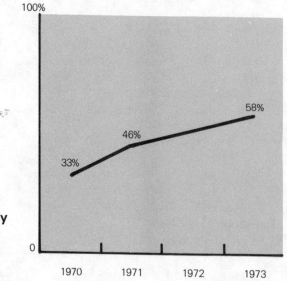

**Economic Security
as an Important
Job Criterion
(College Youth)**

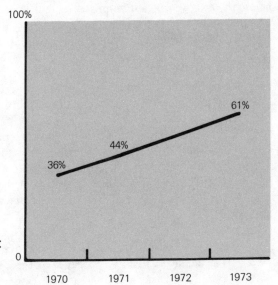

Money You Can Earn as an Important Job Criterion (College Youth)

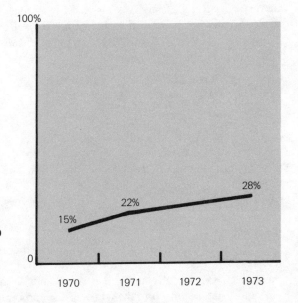

Prestige of the Job as an Important Criterion (College Youth)

heterogeneous, we are not surprised to find that more than one pattern of adaption and synthesis has begun to emerge. One such pattern emphasizes the New Values, pushing conventional career considerations to a side. This pattern is most characteristic of the large group of college students who take affluence for granted. We have referred to this group throughout the report as the take-affluence-for-granted segment—an awkward but descriptive label. This group now represents about one out of every three college students (34 percent).

At the other extreme is a group who stress the practical and pragmatic side of education and career. Their main concern is with economic security and the extrinsic rewards of a career in the form of money, status, economic security, etc. They comprise about 35 percent of today's total college population. The remaining 32 percent are, in a sense, the most interesting. They are the young people who put a strong emphasis on the intangibles of self-fulfillment and self-actualization and yet, at the same time, their major purpose in going to college is for practical career training. They strike what is perhaps the dominant theme of today's college climate: they are trying to achieve a synthesis between the old and the new values by assuming that it is possible to seek and find self-fulfillment and personal satisfaction in a conventional career, while simultaneously enjoying the kind of financial rewards that will enable them to live full, rich lives outside of their work. The job criteria they stress put equal emphasis on challenging work, the ability to express one's self, and free time for outside interests, as well as on the money one can earn, economic security, and the chance to get ahead.

"Bargain" with Society

This effort to integrate new values with traditional ones illustrates one of the central issues in social science. The process of socialization, as it is called, refers to the extraordinarily complex process whereby the individual seeks to adapt himself to the institutions of the society while at the same time hoping to modify those institutions so that they meet his needs more fully. One of the striking differences between the adaptions of college-educated young people in the 1950s and college-educated young people today is seen in the nature of the "bargain" these young people make with the society.

In the 1950s, the era of privatism and togetherness, many young people felt that it was necessary to split their lives in two as a means of adjusting to the society. On the job, they placed their emphasis on getting ahead, making out, and living according to the mores of the corporate structure. (The classic stereotype of this era was the man in the gray flannel suit.) The other side of life came on holidays, weekends, and evenings. It was then one retreated from the public world to one's private world—to suburbs, home, garden, station wagon, kids, and family. A rigid mental wall separated that part of one's self that belonged to the world from the other part of one's self that belonged to family, friends, and private life. The purpose of the rigid compartmentalization was to satisfy both the demands of the society and one's own personal cravings. One of the defining characteristics of that earlier era was that young people found it necessary to compartmentalize their lives in order to adjust to the society. In no other way could the individual see how to reconcile the conflicting demands of the society with his own yearnings.

Today, this compartmentalization no longer operates. The nature of the "bargain" young people make with society does not require them to split themselves down the middle. They do not feel caught up in a sharp dichotomy between private and social values. They do not accept the need to submerge their "real selves" in their work while adopting a completely different set of values in their private lives. This is a change of some importance. It is a change, moreover, that has occurred both in the psychology of college youth and in the psychology of the larger society as well. Increasingly, the older generation has begun to move toward the value structure of young people. There is growing recognition in the business world of the appeal of nonfinancial rewards, participation in decision making, tolerance of varied styles of dress and outlook, and an effort to make work interesting and meaningful. Even as college students are pausing to consolidate their views and values and to synthesize them with traditional career goals, they can see evidence all around them that the desire for personal self-fulfillment and the desire for a successful career need not be incompatible. In the future, as a result of this shift, we may expect the very concept of career and professionalism to change in meaning, in subtle but far-reaching ways.

The picture of college youth in relation to society that emerges from the research is touched with irony. Just a few years ago, the country was reduced to near panic by what seemed to be the wholesale alienation of college youth. Now we find an almost classic formula for accommodation and adaption. Most college students accept the necessity for hard work as a fact of life. They do not shirk it or shrink from it. At the same time what they regard as a proper payoff for hard work has shifted dramatically.

Students specifically reject a nose-to-the-grindstone philosophy of life. They do not subscribe to the old credo that if they work hard, stay out of trouble, and put their responsibilities to family and others ahead of their own personal satisfactions, then they will be rewarded with a good living, economic security, enough money to buy possessions, a nice place to live, and a good education for their kids. What we see instead is the active pursuit of a career as a means to self-fulfillment, with money, security, and possessions included in the overall scheme, partly taken for granted, partly demanded as a matter of right, but subordinate to the main goal of finding just the right life style for expressing their psychological potential.

Shifting from a psychological to a sociological point of view, we see a growing majority of college-trained youth readying themselves for careers in the upper reaches of the social order. The professional, managerial, and technical categories are the fastest growing occupational groupings in the country. These prestigious positions will make hard demands on people's trained capabilities, their willingness to respond to challenge, and their ability to adapt to innovation. How convenient it is, then, that increasing numbers of young people are heading straight for these upper level niches, their eyes fixed on the goal marked "successful career." Moreover, they are demanding that these careers be meaningful and rewarding in both psychological and economic senses. Fortunately for them, it appears that there will be an abundance of such careers available. Today's students are training themselves for positions in an elite group which is peculiarly necessary in an advanced industrial society.

From this standpoint, even though these well-educated young adults may be searching for more varied life styles than their parents did, the celebrated generation gap in any profound sense, disappears before our eyes. Other Yankelovich research shows that in the country today the most satisfied group—those who are most at ease with the society as it exists, the most pleased with their work, gratified with their income, and content with their own personal lives—are the upper-middle-class families that occupy the leading professional, managerial, and technical positions in the society. Looking at the future prospects for this large and growing social class, the "fit" between aspiration and opportunity appears exceptionally good. It is precisely this kind of good fit between values and institutions that makes for institutional legitimacy and stability.

This optimistic view of the relationship of college-educated youth to their future work dramatizes, by contrast, the plight of the majority of young people who either receive no college education at all, or have one or two years of college before dropping out. This is the situation for three out of four young people, since at the present time about one out of four persons, age eighteen to twenty-five, finishes four years of college. It is to this group that we now turn.

3

THE NONCOLLEGE MAJORITY

FOLLOWING THE CAMPUS

Perhaps the single most striking finding of the study is the extent to which
the gap between college and noncollege youth has closed over these past six
years. What we find today is an astonishingly swift transmission of values
formerly confined to a minority of college youth and now spread throughout
the generation. This is not to say that noncollege youth have arrived at
precisely the same value orientations as their college peers. What the research
does show, to an almost uncanny degree, is that noncollege youth today is
just about where the college population was in 1969. Virtually every aspect

of the New Values have deeply penetrated noncollege youth. Moral norms have changed dramatically. Social values with regard to money, work, and family are slowly being transformed. And the same intangible conflict between self-fulfillment and economic security is spreading throughout every group in the youth population. The series of charts that follow illustrate this conclusion. The first group of charts compares three findings: (1) how college students felt in 1969, (2) how the noncollege group felt in 1969, and (3) how the noncollege group feels today. The later group compares two findings: (1) how the college group feels today and (2) how the noncollege group feels today. The first series of charts shows changing moral norms, the second series shows changing social values.

CHANGING MORAL NORMS

1. **Sexual Morality**
2. **Religion**
3. **Patriotism**

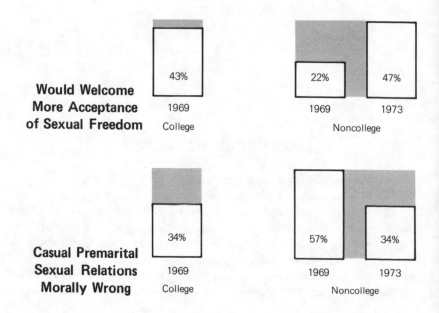

Would Welcome More Acceptance of Sexual Freedom

43% — 1969 College

22% — 1969 / 47% — 1973 Noncollege

Casual Premarital Sexual Relations Morally Wrong

34% — 1969 College

57% — 1969 / 34% — 1973 Noncollege

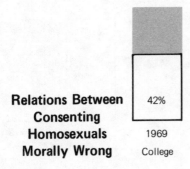

Relations Between Consenting Homosexuals Morally Wrong

42%
1969
College

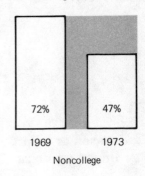

72%
1969

47%
1973

Noncollege

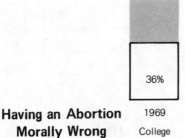

Having an Abortion Morally Wrong

36%
1969
College

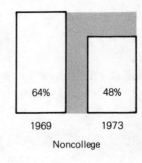

64%
1969

48%
1973

Noncollege

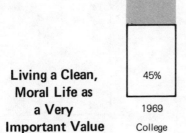

Living a Clean, Moral Life as a Very Important Value

45%
1969
College

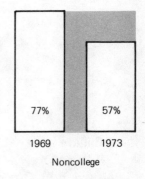

77%
1969

57%
1973

Noncollege

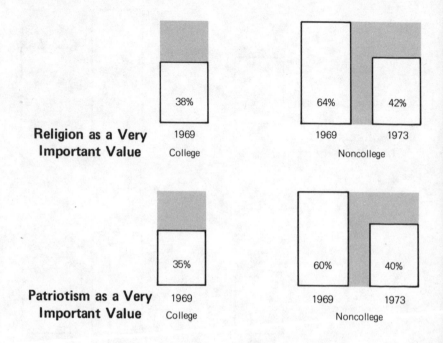

**Religion as a Very
Important Value**

38%
1969
College

64%   42%
1969   1973
Noncollege

**Patriotism as a Very
Important Value**

35%
1969
College

60%   40%
1969   1973
Noncollege

CHANGING SOCIAL VALUES

1. Work
2. Money
3. Family

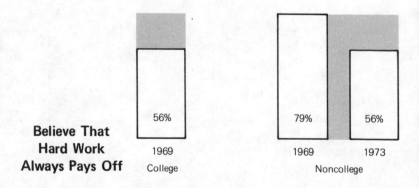

**Believe That
Hard Work
Always Pays Off**

56%
1969
College

79%   56%
1969   1973
Noncollege

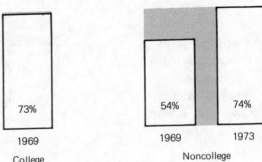

**Would Welcome
Less Emphasis
on Money**

**Keeping Feelings
Under Control as a
Very Important
Quality in a Man
1973**

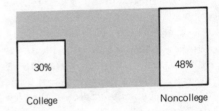

**Being a
Good Provider as a
Very Important
Quality in a Man
1973**

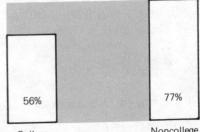

**Putting Family
Before Anything
Else as a
Very Important
Quality in a Man
1973**

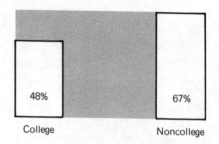

48%

College

67%

Noncollege

NEW ATTITUDES TOWARD WORK

Dilemma for Noncollege Youth Created by New Values

In an earlier section we showed how the New Values spread from a college minority to the career-minded majority of college youth. We described how today's college youth were attempting to find a constructive synthesis between traditional and new values. And we suggested that their efforts were likely to meet with success on the grounds that there appears to be a "good fit" between what these young people want and what the society has to offer its college-educated youth. The same conclusion cannot be advanced about the impact of the New Values on noncollege youth. Without the benefits of a college education, the opportunities to find work that is both financially and psychologically rewarding are not very great—and most young people know it.

The noncollege majority recognize that they are less likely than college-trained people to find interesting work. In the past, this did not matter too much. Most people looked to work for its extrinsic rewards—good pay, a mounting standard of living, economic security. But gradually, the New Values and a sense of personal entitlement are seeping into the consciousness of all young people, not just college youth.

The summary points and charts that follow describe the changing values and attitudes of young people toward the world of work, as revealed by the current research.

New Stress on Quality of Life

Traditionally in American life, especially among working people, success has meant money, economic security, status, and social mobility for one's children. Today, many noncollege youth, including those working in blue-collar jobs, have taken up the quest of their college peers for a new definition of success in which the emphasis is on self-fulfillment and quality of life, as well as on money and security.

Some indications of the trend:

While a majority (57 percent) of noncollege youth state that economic security and providing for their family will come first in planning their future, a substantial minority (42 percent) agree with the following statement: "In thinking about the future, I'm really not that concerned with economic security. I guess I take it for granted. I'm more concerned with doing things that will give me a sense of self-fulfillment." With the New Values spreading so quickly it is a fair assumption that this 42 percent is likely to increase, perhaps even to the 56 percent "self-fulfillment comes first" levels now prevailing among college youth.

Among young blue-collar workers "interesting work" is just as important a desired job attribute as money.

Today, three out of four of both college and noncollege youth call for more emphasis on self-expression and self-fulfillment as personal values.

Less Concern About Money and Economic Security

Certainly there is no indication that young workers are willing to sacrifice economic gains for self-fulfillment. The change that appears to be occurring is the emphasis on rewards that go beyond economic security. For increasing numbers of young workers money by itself is no longer enough of an incentive for hard work.

While economic security continues to dominate their lives, many young people have begun to take it for granted. If they are working, the future prospect that they might be unable to make a living seems curiously unreal. For example, among young people who are now employed, 58 percent have no doubt about their being able to make as much money as they want to—whatever that amount is. Perhaps the energy crisis will slow this trend down—but it appears unlikely, as some assume, to be wiped away by a changed economy.

The appeal of a job that is more than just a job is demonstrated in the findings of the study.

Among blue-collar workers, job security (51 percent) is 15 percentage points below interesting work as a job criterion.

Out of a list of thirty-five possible job criteria, the chance to make a *lot* of money ranks among the bottom ten on the list.

The job criteria of blue-collar workers are remarkably similar to those of the college students and the young college graduates already in the work force. What they want is no longer just satisfactory pay or job security, but also the opportunity to do self-rewarding and interesting work. The two most important criteria to young blue-collar workers are interesting work (66 percent) and good pay (65 percent).

Positive Attitudes Toward Work

Young working people, regardless of the nature of their work, say they are ready to work hard. They definitely are not looking for work that is not demanding. They do not shirk from physically hard work, and they are not worried about being asked to do more than they now do. But the nature of the "payoff" for hard work has changed. In 1969, 79 percent of the non-college youth believed that "hard work would always pay off," a view held by only 57 percent of college youth. Now the same traditional feeling about

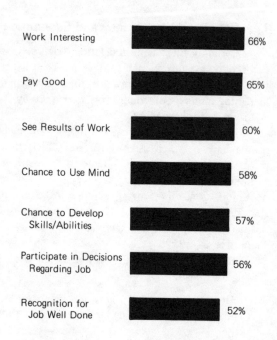

Work Interesting — 66%

Pay Good — 65%

See Results of Work — 60%

Chance to Use Mind — 58%

Chance to Develop Skills/Abilities — 57%

Participate in Decisions Regarding Job — 56%

Recognition for Job Well Done — 52%

Most Important Job Attributes Among Blue-Collar Workers 1973

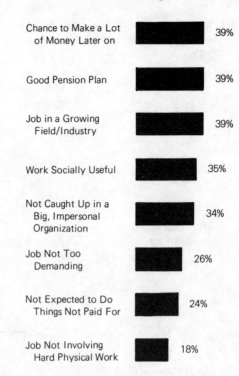

Chance to Make a Lot of Money Later on	39%
Good Pension Plan	39%
Job in a Growing Field/Industry	39%
Work Socially Useful	35%
Not Caught Up in a Big, Impersonal Organization	34%
Job Not Too Demanding	26%
Not Expected to Do Things Not Paid For	24%
Job Not Involving Hard Physical Work	18%

Least Important Job Attributes Among Blue-Collar Workers 1973

hard work as the royal road to success is supported by only 56 percent of noncollege youth. A note should be made, however, that a strong majority of *both* college and noncollege youth continue to reject, at 1969 levels, the idea of less emphasis on working hard. In other words, young people are *willing* to work hard, but they have lost their confidence in hard work paying off in terms of psychological as well as economic rewards.

Limited Job Satisfaction

The difference between the personal rewards and satisfactions found at work by college-educated young people and blue-collar workers points to one of the major disparities in our society.

The young professional or executive sees his work as providing him with not only a good future, but also with the opportunity to use his skills and intelligence and to do work that is meaningful and rewarding. The young blue-collar worker often brings to the job many of the same desires for rewarding work that demands the use of his brains, full resources, and creativity. In many instances, however, unlike the young executive or professional, he finds a job that is "just a job"—a way to kill time and make a living.

The contrast in job attitudes of blue-collar workers and young executives is made dramatically clear in the following charts.

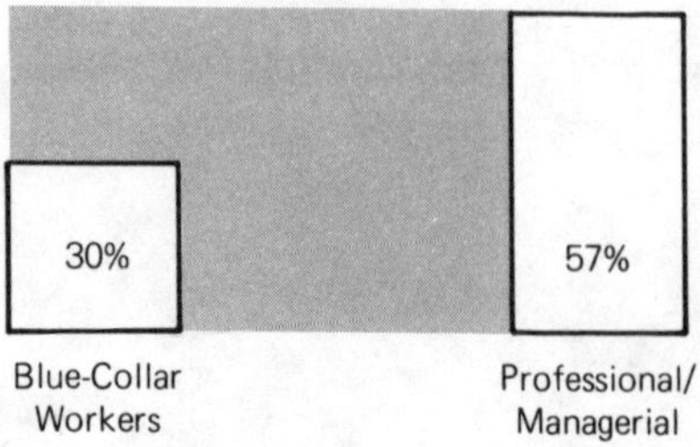

**It's a Job
with a Good Future
1973**

30%	57%
Blue-Collar Workers	Professional/ Managerial

**I'm Just Hanging on
Until Something
Better Comes Along
1973**

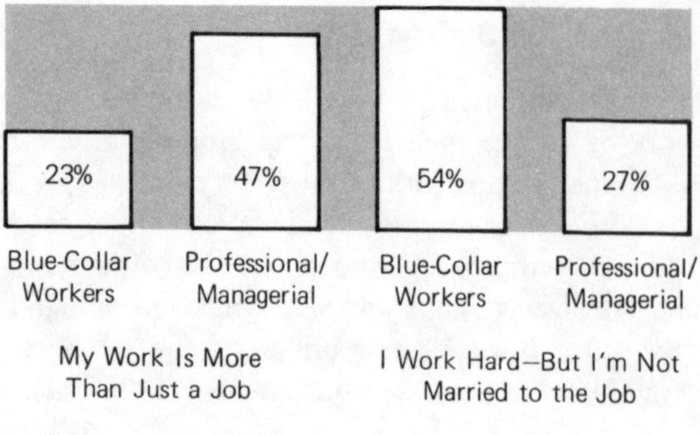

31%	11%
Blue-Collar Workers	Professional/ Managerial

**Relationship to
Present Job
1973**

23%	47%	54%	27%
Blue-Collar Workers	Professional/ Managerial	Blue-Collar Workers	Professional/ Managerial
My Work Is More Than Just a Job		I Work Hard—But I'm Not Married to the Job	

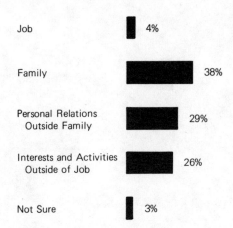

**Sources of
Satisfaction Among
Blue-Collar Workers
1973**

Job	4%
Family	38%
Personal Relations Outside Family	29%
Interests and Activities Outside of Job	26%
Not Sure	3%

Education One Answer

The intensity and universality of the desire for more education and training, undoubtedly one of the key findings of the study, reflects the main strategy expressed by noncollege youth for dealing constructively with their present and future job frustrations, and their readiness to do something positive about it if given the opportunity.

Forty-five percent see their educational background as the major barrier toward getting the kind of work wanted.

Thirty-seven percent regard their lack of vocational training as an impediment to the kind of job wanted.

Given the opportunity to get a six-month training or education program which would lead to a promotion or better job elsewhere, 68 percent say they would welcome the chance, even if it meant taking a 20 percent pay cut while taking the course. It would be naive to take this finding literally, as a prediction of future behavior. But the finding is important in what it says about attitudes and values.

Alternatives to College or Work

A boy or girl graduating from high school today has two alternatives—to go to work (which for some means to enlist in the Armed Forces) or to go on to college, either a two-year or a four-year college. For some, however, there is not even this alternative—due to money problems, intellectual limitations, family needs, etc.

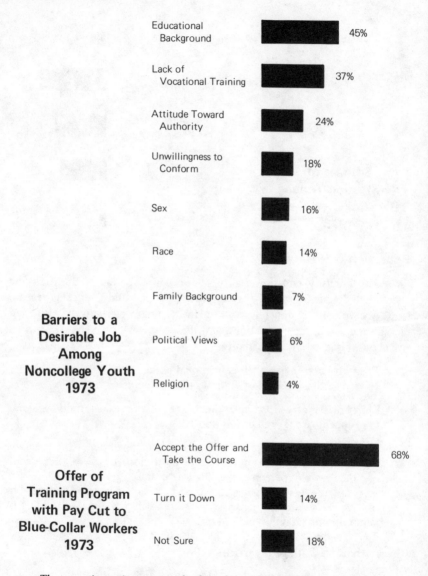

**Barriers to a
Desirable Job
Among
Noncollege Youth
1973**

Educational Background — 45%
Lack of Vocational Training — 37%
Attitude Toward Authority — 24%
Unwillingness to Conform — 18%
Sex — 16%
Race — 14%
Family Background — 7%
Political Views — 6%
Religion — 4%

**Offer of
Training Program
with Pay Cut to
Blue-Collar Workers
1973**

Accept the Offer and Take the Course — 68%
Turn it Down — 14%
Not Sure — 18%

The question arises as to whether these alternatives can be made more flexible. Is there an opportunity for new institutions that would be more responsive to the needs of young people?

In this connection we pretested five concepts that posed alternatives to the present limited work-versus-college choice.

Plan I. A start-your-own-business program would feature training and interest-free loans.

Plan II. New types of technical schools would offer certified training for skills needed in expanding industries.

Plan III. A career-planning year would expose the individual to many different fields and job opportunities and feature new forms of career counseling.

Plan IV. New types of apprenticeship programs in industry, the arts, unions, or service organizations would offer the individual minimum wages while he learns new skills.

Plan V. A six-year job-and-college program would involve working steadily at a job and receiving a college degree for both work and formal courses taken at a nearby college.

Asked how they would react to each of these alternatives if they were graduating from high school today, here is how the blue-collar workers responded:

Seventy-six percent said they would give serious thought to a career-planning year.

Seventy-one percent would give serious consideration to the six-year combined job-and-college program.

Sixty-eight percent expressed interest in the new types of technical schools.

Sixty-six percent were interested in the new types of apprenticeship programs.

Fifty-five percent reacted favorably to the start-your-own-business program.

Interestingly, college students share the blue-collar workers' enthusiasm for the career-planning year and the six-year work-college program, but are somewhat less interested in the start-your-own-business program or in the new types of technical schools. The following chart shows the response of the total young adult population to these five concepts.

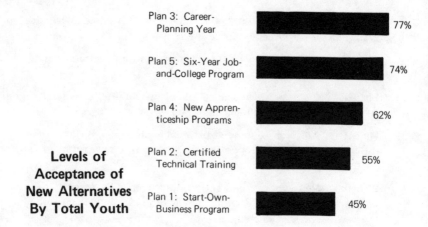

Levels of Acceptance of New Alternatives By Total Youth

Plan 3: Career-Planning Year — 77%

Plan 5: Six-Year Job-and-College Program — 74%

Plan 4: New Apprenticeship Programs — 62%

Plan 2: Certified Technical Training — 55%

Plan 1: Start-Own-Business Program — 45%

Whether, indeed, today's young adults would take advantage of such programs and alternatives if they were available is open to question. Our own interpretation is that the desire for taking advantage of these new opportunities, if they existed, is strongly buttressed by the value structure and emerging cultural patterns of a "new" generation of Americans. Perhaps the more fundamental question is, What will happen if these needs are not met?

Minority Youth

Not surprisingly, it is minority youth who feel most left out. Only a small percentage go on to college: dropouts from high school are twice as numerous among black and other minority youth as among their white peers. Among minority youth, the prevailing view is that this society is sick (55 percent) and not democratic (76 percent). They are disheartened by what they feel is rampant racism. They are having problems making ends meet and, unlike their white peers, are also doubtful about their future ability to make money.

Minority youth are caught in an acute dilemma by the New Values. On the one hand, they endorse the freer, more open kind of relationships and life styles promoted by the New Values; on the other hand, they are personally more concerned than other young people with education, work, and money.

SUMMING UP THE SITUATION

Work that provides psychological as well as economic benefits is as attractive to the nation's young high school graduates as to its college graduates—but they do not really expect to get it from their jobs. Upward mobility is also important to them, but opportunities for mobility and for job enrichment are often traded away in exchange for economic benefits. At the same time, opportunities for skilled workers in industrial jobs may be shrinking. Low-level service jobs, which are growing in number, often lead to a dead end. Information about good jobs open to the person without a college education is difficult to acquire. The opportunities for training, apprenticeship, and the acquisition of new skills are sporadic, all too often poorly conceived, and do not look to most young people as if they will produce results.

Today's generation of young people is less fearful of economic insecurity than generations in the past. They want interesting and challenging work, but they assume that their employers cannot—or will not—provide it. By their own say-so, they are inclined to take "less crap" than older workers. They are not as automatically loyal to the organization as their fathers, and they are far more cognizant of their own needs and rights. Nor are they as awed by organizational and hierarchical authority. Being less fearful of "discipline" and the threat of losing their jobs, they feel free to express their discontent in myriad ways, from fooling around on the job to sabotage. They are better educated than their parents, even without a college degree. They want more freedom and opportunity and will struggle hard to achieve it.

That the majority of noncollege youth face the prospect of growing difficulties with their jobs must be regarded as a matter of serious concern to the society. These young people, after all, represent the great bulk of the new labor force. The problem they face is compounded by the multiplier effect of higher expectations with lower opportunities: their New Values inevitably clash with the built-in rigidities and limited responses of the traditional work place.

A word of caution is in order here. It is important not to overstate the implications of the research. A disgruntled, discontented work force of high school graduates, uninterested in their jobs and eager to cut back on work commitments irrespective of economic rewards, is far from inevitable. Conversely, however, the conventional view of a future work force contented simply because they are making a good living and improving their material standard of life is even more unlikely. We are reaching one of those critical turning-points in our social history where the options of the future and the opportunities to create new institutions are truly open. The die is not yet cast. The majority of young people continue to bring to their work a deeply rooted desire to do a good job and a hunger for work that will satisfy some of their deepest cravings—for community, for fellowship, for participation, for challenge, for self-fulfillment, for freedom, and for equality.

4
WOMEN'S LIBERATION

The study findings contain a wealth of information about the attitudes of young people toward Women's Liberation (see Chapter 9). The findings show that these ideas have had their warmest reception on the nation's campuses. This is not surprising since there is a close connection between the ideas of the Women's Liberation Movement with its stress on self-fulfillment for women and the core concepts of the New Values.

The findings show that a majority of young people today, both college and noncollege, believe that women should receive equal pay for equal work, that women should be free to take the initiative in matters of sex, that men and women share the same essential human nature (in striking contrast to Freud's dictum that anatomy is destiny), and that women's relationships to other women are just as important as their relationships to men. On the other hand, a majority reject the idea that women can do almost any job as well as men can and that women do not need men to be happy. Young adults are equally divided on whether women are just as logical as men and whether the old saw about the woman's place in the home is, or is not, nonsense.

MEASURES OF A MAN

The chart that follows shows how young adults (college and non-college) define what it means to be a man. The reader will note that being physically strong, good looking in a masculine way, handy around the house,

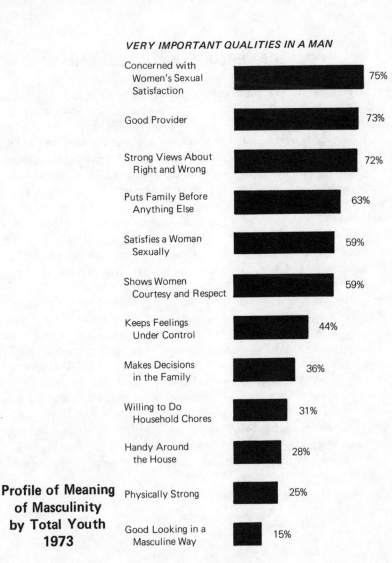

VERY IMPORTANT QUALITIES IN A MAN

Quality	Percent
Concerned with Women's Sexual Satisfaction	75%
Good Provider	73%
Strong Views About Right and Wrong	72%
Puts Family Before Anything Else	63%
Satisfies a Woman Sexually	59%
Shows Women Courtesy and Respect	59%
Keeps Feelings Under Control	44%
Makes Decisions in the Family	36%
Willing to Do Household Chores	31%
Handy Around the House	28%
Physically Strong	25%
Good Looking in a Masculine Way	15%

Profile of Meaning of Masculinity by Total Youth 1973

and willing to do household chores are not regarded as important elements of masculinity by very many young people. The three major components of masculinity that head the list are (1) the man's concern with the woman's sexual satisfaction, (2) his ability to be a good economic provider, and (3) his readiness to hold strong moral views about what is right and what is wrong.

COLLEGE VERSUS NONCOLLEGE WOMEN

Perhaps the key point about Women's Liberation ideas in relation to today's youth is that they have created a wide schism between women in college and women who do not have a college education. Women college students eagerly embrace the New Values associated with Women's Liberation, in part, because they see their way clear to combine marriage with a self-fulfilling career. Here, once again, the diffusion of New Values poses an acute social dilemma to the young women who lack a college education. For this latter group, work is not a self-fulfilling career but a job to help make ends meet. The majority of young noncollege women who are married devote their lives to the role of housewife and mother. For these women, many of the new Women's Liberation ideas, with their stress on self-fulfillment through career and work, pose a serious threat to self-esteem and to traditional beliefs.

There are, therefore, at least two large groups of women in the youth population who feel less than easy with the New Values. One is composed of blue-collar working women who have the least satisfying jobs and the least opportunity to get better ones. They find it difficult to identify with their college sisters who stress self-realization through the job. The other group consists of housewives who gladly accept the role of housewife and who feel threatened by the doubts that have been raised about a woman's ability to achieve her full potential through motherhood and wifehood.

The charts that follow illustrate the enormity of the gap between college and noncollege women on a wide range of beliefs associated with the New Values and the ideas promulgated by the Women's Liberation Movement.

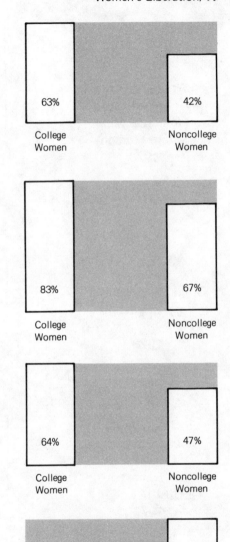

**Women Are
Discriminated
Against
1973**

63% — College Women

42% — Noncollege Women

**Women Should Be
Free to Take the
Initiative in Sex
1973**

83% — College Women

67% — Noncollege Women

**"Women's Place
Is in the Home"
Is Nonsense
1973**

64% — College Women

47% — Noncollege Women

**Having Children
Without Formal
Marriage Is
Morally Wrong
1973**

41% — College Women

62% — Noncollege Women

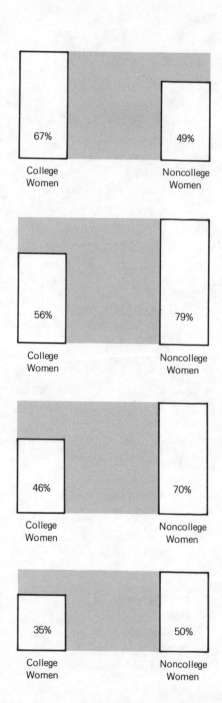

Women Are as Important to Women as Men Are to Women 1973

67% College Women

49% Noncollege Women

Being a Good Provider as a Very Important Quality in a Man 1973

56% College Women

79% Noncollege Women

Putting Family Before Anything Else as a Very Important Quality in a Man 1973

46% College Women

70% Noncollege Women

Having Children as a Very Important Value 1973

35% College Women

50% Noncollege Women

Showing Women Courtesy and Respect as a Very Important Quality in a Man 1973

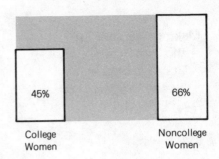

Casual Premarital Sex Relations Morally Wrong 1973

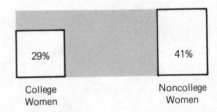

Living a Clean, Moral Life as a Very Important Value 1973

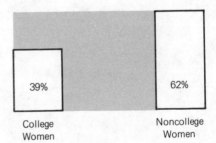

Keeping Feelings Under Control as a Very Important Quality in a Man 1973

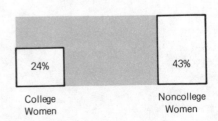

**Making Decisions in
the Family as a
Very Important
Quality in a Man
1973**

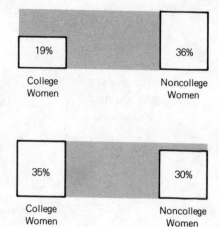

College
Women

Noncollege
Women

**Willingness to Do
Household Chores as
a Very Important
Quality in a Man
1973**

5
POLITICAL SKEPTICS

"SPECIAL INTERESTS" RUN THE NATION

The most subtle and difficult implications of the findings are those that relate to politics and political viewpoints. The surface facts are easy to summarize. The vast majority of young people today, approximately three out of four college and noncollege young adults, express considerable personal satisfaction with the way their personal life is going. They say they are enjoying life, they feel they have good opportunities for the future, they want more education, and two out of three state that they are able to make ends meet. A large majority say they have no insuperable problem in accepting the conventional life styles offered by the society, expressing their belief that our society as it exists today is essentially healthy and its problems manageable.

At the same time, however, more than six out of ten young adults today believe that the society is democratic in name only. They believe that "special interests" run the political machinery of the nation, with little true participation by the mass of American citizens. Four out of five are critical of the nation's foreign policy, and predict that involvements similar to Vietnam are inevitable. Fewer than one out of five (9 percent of the college students and 15 percent of the noncollege population) feel that we ended the Vietnam War with honor. (The majority believe either that we could have achieved the same end result earlier or that we brought dishonor on the nation.) More than 90 percent of all young people hold that business is too concerned with its own profits and insufficiently concerned with serving the public. Criticism of business and political parties have grown by leaps and bounds in the past few years, especially among noncollege youth. In 1969, 44 percent of the noncollege group believed that our political parties needed fundamental change. Today, 64 percent hold this belief. In 1969, 24 percent of noncollege youth believed that big business required fundamental reform. Today that proportion has almost doubled to 45 percent. It is not surprising, therefore, that the "special interests" that the majority of young people see as dominating the political process turn out to be big business and politicians concerned with their own welfare rather than with the interests of the public. Despite the feelings of personal well-being, we find widespread skepticism about the political process.

Fewer than half of the noncollege population voted in the last election, their votes split equally between Mr. McGovern and Mr. Nixon. Three out of four college students said they voted in the last election, with McGovern given a 4 to 3 edge over Nixon in the distribution of the campus vote. By more than 2 to 1 margins, young people align themselves with the Democratic Party over the Republican Party. Almost half the college youth (45 percent) say they are Democrats, while 21 percent claim allegiance to the Republican Party. Among noncollege youth, 49 percent are Democrats and 24 percent are Republicans. Twice as many college youth as noncollege (23 percent to 12 percent) characterize themselves as being actively interested and involved in political matters. In the college population, more than half of all students describe themselves as being one or another shade of liberal (53 percent), 21 percent are completely middle-of-the-road, 21 percent are conservative, and 5 percent are radical. The pattern among the noncollege population is similar but with more conservatives and fewer liberals.

On controversial political issues, the noncollege majority are decidedly more conservative than their college cohorts. More of them favor the death penalty for certain crimes (52 percent to 44 percent), more of them favor life sentences for drug pushers (45 percent to 30 percent), fewer of them favor legalizing marijuana (47 percent to 60 percent), and fewer of them favor granting amnesty to draft evaders (42 percent to 52 percent).

Here, too, on the political front the gap within the generation between college students and the noncollege majority has narrowed. College students have become somewhat more conservative over the past few years and pay more credence to the importance of law and order, while the noncollege group has, in certain respects, become somewhat less conservative.

Other research conducted by the Yankelovich organization shows that the political center in the nation as a whole has shifted toward a greater conservatism.[1] This same generalization cannot be applied to the nation's young people. Their political views appear to be in a greater state of flux, with no clear-cut direction as yet.

Bill of New Rights

Perhaps the most important political question for the future relates to the outcome of the effort by the noncollege majority to satisfy their new values and expectations within the structure of existing work and educational institutions. The present mood of the majority is upbeat, but this generation of young people has fairly high expectations and a strong sense of entitlement. They are developing a broad new agenda of social rights. By social rights we mean the psychological process whereby a person's wants and desires become converted into a set of presumed rights.

In the past, Social Security, medical insurance, Medicaid, unemployment insurance, all started out as "wants" and have now become institutionalized as "rights." Similarly today, noncollege youth are almost on a par with their college peers in their rising expectations regarding their right to:

Send children to college whether or not they can afford to do so.

Participate in decisions that affect their work.

Enjoy a secure retirement.

Have access to the best medical care whether they can afford it or not.

The Future

One can only begin to speculate what this new, intense expression of social rights among young people will mean in the way of social change in the future. The concept of social rights has always exerted a strong force in our society, and in recent years, a number of institutional forms have sprung up

[1]Studies conducted for *Time* magazine, 1973.

that have shortened the time span between the individual's sense of entitlement and political action. In the 1960's, a variety of social movements came into being—the Civil Rights Movement, the Consumer Movement, the Women's Movement, the Ecology Movement, etc. These movements have served to articulate, define, and shape a full agenda of new social rights. An important question today is what young people will do with an expanded Bill of Rights so closely tied to the New Values.

The research shows that beneath the surface of contentment expressed by noncollege youth are a number of small signs of growing resentment against groups who appear, in their eyes, to be getting something for nothing (e.g., welfare recipients, students, minority groups). The great bulk of the nation's young people are not politicized in the same sense in which the working-class youth in South American and European countries are. Their hopes are high, their outlook is sanguine and, for the most part, is private, personal, and nonpolitical. But they have now begun to develop a more critical view of the society (similar to their college counterparts), and they feel a growing resentment toward those who do not live by the rules they so willingly accept. If America's work, education, and political institutions prove to be flexible and responsive, we can look forward to a period of social stability, moderation in politics, and perhaps even a resurgence of traditional American optimism about the future. If, however, these institutions prove rigid and unresponsive and our political leadership shows insensitivity to the changing needs and values of our youth, then the underlying potential for discontent will become all too real and we will face a period of instability and demagoguery.

The charts that follow show selective findings that illustrate some of the points made in this section.

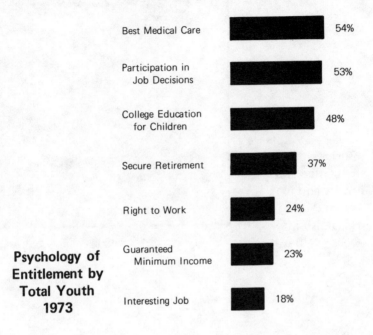

ENTITLED TO AS A SOCIAL RIGHT

Best Medical Care — 54%

Participation in Job Decisions — 53%

College Education for Children — 48%

Secure Retirement — 37%

Right to Work — 24%

Guaranteed Minimum Income — 23%

Interesting Job — 18%

Psychology of Entitlement by Total Youth 1973

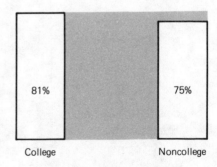

Have Good Opportunities for Future 1973

College 81% Noncollege 75%

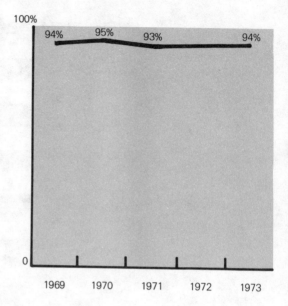

Business Too Concerned with Profits and Not with Public Responsibility (College Youth)

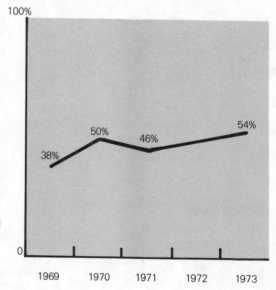

Big Business Needing Fundamental Reform (College Youth)

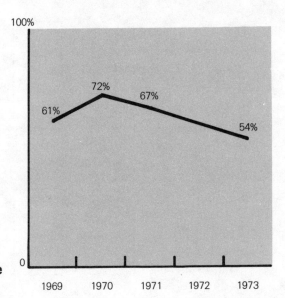

Military Needing Fundamental Change (College Youth)

Too Much Concern for College Students and Not Enough for Other Young People Who Have to Make a Living 1973

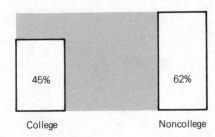

Too Much Concern with Welfare "Bums" and Not Enough for Hard-Working Persons 1973

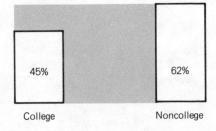

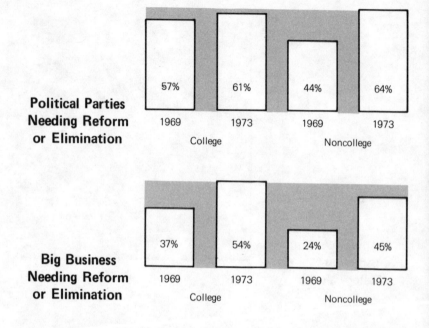

**Political Parties
Needing Reform
or Elimination**

57% 1969 — College
61% 1973 — College
44% 1969 — Noncollege
64% 1973 — Noncollege

**Big Business
Needing Reform
or Elimination**

37% 1969 — College
54% 1973 — College
24% 1969 — Noncollege
45% 1973 — Noncollege

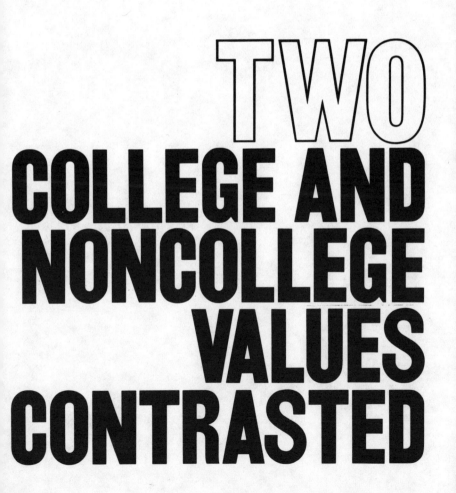

TWO
COLLEGE AND NONCOLLEGE VALUES CONTRASTED

THE CAMPUS AS PACESETTER

6

To understand the present values and attitudes of young people, it is useful to take a step backwards and review the enormous changes that have occurred on the college scene in the short space of a dozen years. Since the early 1960s, the American college campus has gone through four distinct phases.

Phase I—Social Radicalism. The first stage took place in the early years of the decade of the 1960s and was most vividly symbolized by the Free Speech Movement at Berkeley. It was just a decade ago that students were demonstrating on the California campus for the right to use four-letter words. Far more than obscene language was at stake, however, for it was during this period that a pattern of new social values started to emerge on campus. Students began to evaluate tradi-

55

tional American beliefs and to stress new forms of expression, a less conventional life style, freedom to dress and live the way they wanted, and the right to be "yourself" and "tell it like it is." This was a period of what might be called *social radicalism*, as distinct from political radicalism. The focus was on making radical changes in individual life styles, not on political change.

Phase II—The Vietnam War.   Next came the Vietnam War and the move to political radicalism which developed and flourished side by side with the new social radicalism. Superficially, the two movements appeared to be one major thrust, with many social commentators, such as Revel[1] and Reich[2], mistakenly coupling the political and social revolution and evaluating the two separate trends as a single phenomenon.

What actually occurred on the campus, as the Yankelovich 1968 and 1969 studies showed, was that many of the same students (and some different ones) were engrossed in two separate movements—one, the continuation of the search for new life-style values and the other, the militant and often violent protests against an unpopular war and the draft. The tendency to see the two separate and distinct movements as inseparable set the stage for much of the misunderstanding and misinterpretation of the current college scene.

Phase III—The Uncoupling of the Social Values Movement and the Political "Revolution."   As the draft died and the Vietnam War began to ebb, as cease-fire negotiations were undertaken and American soldiers were repatriated, the two movements on the campus (the new social values and the political radicalism) became distinctly uncoupled. The new social values flourished, while political activism and radical identification tied to the draft and the Vietnam War subsided. Campuses suddenly became quieter.

Phase IV—The Era of Synthesis.   Now in 1973 the campus has entered into still another phase—the era of synthesis, in which young people are finding ways to "marry" their new social value system, with its emphasis on self and self-fulfillment, to more traditional career goals.

In examining the changes in students' social and political values since 1968, four major trends can be discerned:

The New Social Values Continue to Grow.   Far from ebbing, the new social value system and the concomitant rejection of traditional

---

[1]Jean-Francois Revel, *Without Marx or Jesus*, Doubleday, New York, 1971.
[2]Charles Reich, *The Greening of America*, Random House, New York, 1970.

values continues to grow on the American campus. From 1968 to the present, there has been a steady upward progression in the percentage of college students who:

Welcome more acceptance of sexual freedom.

Reject materialism for its own sake.

Stress privacy as a personal value.

Reject patriotism, religion, and the traditional view of a "clean, moral life" as important personal values.

Find the present prohibition against marijuana unacceptable.

Are ready to let people live as they want—whether it involves pre-marital sexual relations, homosexuality, etc., without regarding such behavior as a matter of morality.

Question and doubt such traditional American views as putting duty before pleasure, saving money regularly, etc.

The Marriage of New Social Values and Career Goals.   An important finding of the 1973 study is the adaption of the new social values to career goals. In choosing their careers, college students today have come to the conclusion that it is possible to seek and find self-fulfillment and personal satisfaction in their careers while simultaneously seeking the kind of financial rewards that will enable them to live "in style" outside of their work. The synthesis is dramatically documented in the changing pattern of job criteria—with new emphasis on challenging work, the ability to express yourself, and free time for outside interests, alongside of continued concern for the money one can earn, security, and the chance to get ahead.

Another indication of the new careerism is the sharply increased proportion of students who come to college mainly for practical purposes. As mentioned earlier, since 1968 we have divided college students into two major segments—those who regard a college education primarily as a means of advancing their careers, incomes, and social status (career-minded), and those who say they are less concerned with the practical benefits because they take them for granted, and are more concerned with the intangible benefits of a college education (take-affluence-for-granted). The latter group peaked in 1968 and has slowly declined each year since then. Simultaneously, the career-minded segment has increased, with the sharpest acceleration occurring in the last year or so. (See Table 1)

Political Radicalism Peaked in 1970/1971.   Similarly the decline of the political radicalism, which first manifested itself in the 1970 and

1971 surveys, has further eroded in the past two years. Fewer students today than in the past believe that:

This is a sick society.

We are a racist nation.

Violence to achieve worthwhile ends is justifiable.

The police should not use force to maintain order.

The military needs fundamental reform or should be abolished.

The university needs fundamental reform.

Changing society is an important personal value.

Accordingly the tendency among students to describe themselves as "moderates" has increased; the use of the terms "liberal" and "radical" has declined. And students appear to be less alienated than in the past.

Questions About Business and Foreign Policy Continue.   Political radicalism has declined, but not the basic questions about the role of business or the country's foreign policy. From 1969 through 1973, the campus has been almost unanimous in its belief that business is overly concerned with profits at the expense of a proper concern with public responsibility. The issue is not the right of business to make a profit. In 1973 as in 1971, 85 percent of the students believed that business is entitled to a profit. Rather the fundamental question is how well business achieves a good balance between profit and serving the public. In this connection, college students today are more critical of business and more convinced that business needs fundamental reform as an institution than they were even in the peak years of political radicalism.

For easy reference purposes, we have organized the changes that have occurred in college students' views and values since 1968[3] into two major sections: (1) Social and Personal Values, and (2) Political Values.

TRENDS IN SOCIAL AND PERSONAL VALUES

Personal Values Rated as Very Important

Self-fulfillment joins love and friendship as the top-rated values of college students. The most significant changes in the past few years include an increased emphasis on privacy as a very important personal value (up from 64

---

[3]Figures cover the period from the Fall of 1967 (reported in 1968) to the late Spring of 1973.

percent to 71 percent), and a declining commitment to changing society (from 33 percent to 24 percent). (See Table 2)

Sexual Morality

The number of students who say they would welcome greater social acceptance of sexual freedom has increased steadily over the past five years. In 1969, 43 percent of the students looked forward to this change. By 1971, the figure had risen to 56 percent. Now 61 percent want to see a freer, more open sexual morality prevail. Implicit too in the students' support for a freer attitude toward sex is the conviction that in most cases, sexual behavior is an individual decision and not a moral issue. Only a minority of students regard homosexuality as morally wrong (25 percent), abortion (32 percent), casual premarital sexual relations (22 percent), or having children outside of formal marriage (40 percent). For the student majority, these are not moral issues. One of the more dramatic yet typical examples of changes in students' views is their assessment of homosexuality. In 1969, 42 percent considered sexual relations between consenting homosexuals as morally wrong. In 1971 and again in 1973, this view is shared by only one in four students (25 percent). (See Tables 3 and 4)

Marriage and Children

In 1968, only one in four students (24 percent) believed that marriage is an obsolete institution. In the past few years the figure has leveled off at about 32 percent. Today, however, still fewer unmarried students (61 percent) personally look forward to getting married than in 1968 (66 percent). This sentiment, if it continues and is acted upon, would obviously mean a decline in the marriage rate.

Once marriage is involved, however, a majority of students continue to adhere to more traditional views about marital behavior, with approximately the same percentage as in 1971, considering both extramarital sexual relations (60 percent) and partner swapping among couples (57 percent) as morally wrong. (See Tables 4 and 5)

About three out of four college students (76 percent) continue to look forward to having children. Having children, however, is seen as a matter of individual choice—neither a duty to society nor an indispensable life value. Only one out of three students (31 percent)[4] regard having children as a very important personal value. (See Tables 2 and 5)

---

[4]Not asked previously.

Money

On the surface, there is an implicit contradiction in students' views about money. On the one hand, they downgrade it as a personal value, but they also desire to earn as much as they can on the job. What, in fact, the students appear to be saying is that money and possessions should not become an end in themselves or a criteria for judging success. In 1973, 80 percent of the students indicated that they would welcome less emphasis on money, an increase of 4 percent from 1971 (76 percent) and 15 percent since 1968 (65 percent). (See Tables 3 and 9)

Traditional American Values

Part of the New Values Movement has been the increased questioning of many traditional American beliefs. Today, for example, only 54 percent of the college students, compared to 63 percent in 1971, believe in putting duty before pleasure. Similarly, belief that competition encourages excellence has declined from 72 percent in 1969 to 62 percent in both 1971 and this year as well. (See Table 6)

Moral Views

Perhaps as a result of the decline of the political activism of the 1960s and the tactics involved, students today hold stronger moral views than they did previously on questions such as the immorality of taking things without paying for them (84 percent in 1973, 72 percent in 1971) and using violence to achieve worthwhile ends (66 percent to 56 percent). (See Table 4)

Work

There has been a moderate increase in the view that hard work always pays off (44 percent agreement in 1973, 39 percent in 1971). This is still a long way from the 69 percent who held this view several years ago. While the majority of students continue to question the intrinsic rewards of hard work, there is no resistance to hard work as a matter of principal. As in 1971, only 31 percent of all students say they would welcome a society in which less emphasis was placed on working hard, while a large majority (84 percent) believe that it is important to do any job well, no matter how menial. (See Tables 3 and 6)

Career Criteria

While students today place far more emphasis on money as a job criteria than at any other period in the last five years, there is no indication that they are ready to sacrifice any of their previous goals of seeking challenging and socially useful work in order to achieve financial success. Meaningful work, greater financial opportunity, and more free time for outside interests all show an increase this year as important job criteria. (See Table 9)

Future Personal Outlook

Current student attitudes about careers stem from their general value orientations and are not rooted in economic concerns or fears about a job drought. Quite the reverse appears to be the case, with students even more optimistic now about their own abilities to make as much money or to be as successful as they want than they were a few years ago. (See Table 8)

Barriers to Desirable Jobs

A minority of students continue to be troubled about their attitudes toward authority (29 percent) or their unwillingness to conform (28 percent) as possible barriers to getting the kind of job they want. A far more serious worry, however, is on the minds of some students. Almost half (46 percent) of the women students feel that their sex is a formidable barrier to a good job, and two-thirds of the black students (67 percent) feel their race is a barrier. (See Table 10)

Views About Authority

Students' feelings about authority have moderated somewhat over the last few years. Only one in two feel that it is easy for them to accept the power and authority of the police (48 percent) or the power and authority of a "boss" in a work situation (44 percent). On the other hand, more students this year can see themselves as readily accepting outward conformity for the sake of a job (up from 15 percent in 1971 to 20 percent this year), and 32 percent can visualize themselves as more easily settling down to a routine in comparison with the 26 percent who felt this way in the last study. (See Table 7)

Patriotism and Attitudes Toward War

It is still too early to evaluate fully the permanent effects of the Vietnam War on this generation of young people. What is important to note, however, is that even after the war drew to a close, attitudes toward war as a national policy did not change, and the concept of patriotism as a moral value suffered a still further decline. (See Tables 2 and 11)

Drugs

Campus views on drugs support observations by some authorities that the drug problem in college is declining. The prohibition against both heroin and mind-expansion drugs are found more acceptable this year than two years ago. In the case of heroin, 88 percent find this restriction acceptable, and 73 percent accept the restriction on mind-expansion drugs. Only a small minority of students (19 percent) want to see more general acceptance of drug usage. Students draw the line with respect to marijuana. Over the years, the prohibition against marijuana has become increasingly objectionable to college students. In 1968, a majority of all students (55 percent) found the social constraints against marijuana as easily acceptable. Over the course of five years, the number feeling that way has dwindled to 38 percent. (See Table 7)

Life Style

Interest in the commune has waned from the level of interest of two years ago (36 percent). Now only 30 percent of the students say they would be interested in spending at least some time in a communal or collective living situation. On the other hand, an increasing number of students (49 percent) would like to have some opportunity to live in a rural or agricultural situation. In 1971, only 43 percent expressed this interest. (See Table 12)

POLITICAL VALUES—TREND DATA

Blunting of the Radical Diagnosis

In the last two years, the percentage of students who believe that this is a sick society declined from 45 percent to 35 percent. Similarly the belief that our society is too inflexible for change and needs to be abolished fell from 27 percent to 21 percent. There are, however, some indications of a growing sense of distance between government and young people, with slight rises in the proportion of campus youth who believe that this is a democracy in name only (57 percent to 63 percent) and that the real power in the country is vested in the giant corporations and financial institutions (from 77 percent in 1971 to 84 percent this year). (See Tables 13 and 14)

Criticisms of Society

The two aspects of our society which continue to evoke the most consistently severe criticism are the concern of business with profits rather than public responsibility (94 percent) and our foreign policy, which students believe is based on our narrow economic and power interests (88 percent). Considerable concern about the destruction of people's privacy also continues at the same high levels as earlier (86 percent). There has been a gradual diminution in the convictions, but there is still considerable feeling that basically we are a racist nation (79 percent this year, 89 percent in 1970). (See Table 16)

Attitudes Toward Business

One of the most interesting aspects of students' views is their continued respect for the right of business to make a profit, but because of their growing conviction that business strikes a bad balance between profits and public responsibility, they feel that business requires fundamental reform (54 percent now in contrast to 38 percent in 1969). (See Table 15)

Other Institutions Needing Reform

Despite their retreat from political activism, students are still quite critical of the major institutions of American society and government. The penal system, perhaps because of prison turmoil over the past couple of years, has risen to the top of the list of targets for change, with more than two of every three students calling for fundamental reform or abolition. The political parties are not far behind as objects of campus criticism, showing a rise in rejection since 1971 of 54 percent to 61 percent.

Interestingly, the military, a traditional object of student criticism, shows a sustained improvement from earlier years, though a majority continue to call for substantial change (down from 72 percent in 1970 to 67 percent the following year and now at 54 percent). The end of the draft and the cooling of the Vietnam situation has undoubtedly taken some of the heat off the military. Other institutions that are seen as viable by more students now than a few years ago include colleges and universities, mass media, and the Supreme Court. (See Table 15)

Social Justice

The issue of social justice continues to concern college students, although there have been some shifts in emphasis. The American Indians are now regarded by the students as the most oppressed group in the country. In 1971, blacks held this position. The single most outstanding change is the increase in the proportions of students now viewing women as an oppressed group in our society. In 1971, only a third of all students (33 percent) regarded women as discriminated against in our society. Today, under the impact of the Women's Movement and the attention it has received, a majority of college students (58 percent) now consider women as a group that is treated unfairly and discriminated against in our society. (See Table 17)

Political Identification

The year 1970 saw a sharp decline in the number of students who felt a loyalty to either of the major parties. That shift toward unaffiliated status was maintained through the following year, with the Democrats being the biggest losers. Since 1971, however, the major parties, and the Democrats in particular, have more than regained the loyalties of campus youth. In 1973, the Democrats accounted for half of student partisan identification (49 percent), the Republicans got another fourth (24 percent), and the remaining one student in four (27 percent) was not attached to either major party. (See Table 18)

Ideological Self-Perception

Since 1971, there has been a shift away from students classifying themselves as ideologically liberal or radical, with a corresponding rise in the more moderate or liberal/middle-of-the-road positions this year. Student identification with the New Left is sharply off at the same time. Even at the height of the student rebellion, identification with student radicals never exceeded 13 percent to 14 percent. The present drop to 9 percent shows the diminished influence of the most radically oriented groups on campus. (See Table 19)

Alienation

With the end of the war and the growing conviction that society is more ready to listen to and even to adopt their views and values, students appear to be somewhat less alienated this year than in previous years. Four out of ten now feel that their views are shared by most other Americans. In 1969, only a little more than three out of ten shared this same feeling. In addition, a sizable majority (60 percent), compared to 49 percent in 1971, now feel that they will have no great difficulty in accepting the kind of life our society has to offer. (See Table 20)

TABLE 1   CAREER-MINDED VERSUS TAKE-AFFLUENCE-FOR-GRANTED

	Career-Minded %	Take-Affluence-for-Granted %
1973	66	34
1971	61	39
1970	60	40
1969	57	43
1968	55	45

TABLE 2   VERY IMPORTANT PERSONAL VALUES
(College Youth)

	1973 %	1971 %	1970 %	1969 %	1968 %
Love	87	87	*	85	*
Fulfilling yourself as a person	87	*	*	*	*
Friendship	86	87	*	85	*
Education	76	74	*	80	*
Privacy	71	64	*	61	*
Family	68	65	*	*	*
Doing things for others	56	59	*	51	*
Creativity	50	52	*	*	*
Being close to nature	45	47	*	*	*
Work	43	45	*	*	*
Living a clean, moral life	34	34	*	45	*
Having children	31	*	*	*	*
Religion	28	31	*	38	*
Money	20	18	*	18	*
Changing society	24	34	*	33	*
Patriotism	19	27	*	35	*

*Question was not asked.

TABLE 3   WELCOME VALUE CHANGES
(College Youth)

	1973 %	1971 %	1970 %	1969 %	1968 %
More emphasis on self-expression	83	80	*	84	78
Less emphasis on money	80	76	*	73	65
More acceptance of sexual freedom	61	56	*	43	*
More emphasis on technological improvements	55	39	*	56	*
More emphasis on law and order	51	50	*	56	60
More emphasis on traditional family ties	51	45	*	*	*
More respect for authority	48	45	*	59	58
Less emphasis on permissiveness	33	*	*	*	*
Less emphasis on working hard	31	30	*	24	31
More acceptance of drug usage	19	*	*	*	*

*Question was not asked.

TABLE 4 MORAL ISSUES
(College Youth)

Activities Thought to Be Morally Wrong	1973 %	1971 %	1970 %	1969 %	1968 %
Taking things without paying for them	84	78	*	*	*
Destroying private property	78	72	*	*	*
Collecting welfare when you could work	77	75	*	*	*
Using violence to achieve worthwhile ends†	66	56	*	*	*
Paying for college by selling dope	64	63	*	*	*
Extramarital sexual relations	60	57	*	77	*
Interchanging partners among couples	57	59	*	*	*
Cheating big companies	50	*	*	*	*
Living with spouse you do not love	41	*	*	*	*
Having children outside formal marriage	40	42	*	*	*
Having an abortion	32	27	*	36	*
Relations between consenting homosexuals	25	26	*	42	*
Casual premarital sexual relations	22	25	*	34	*

*Question was not asked.

†In 1971 students were asked which of the following statements best expressed their feelings about the use of violence:
  a. Violent means are often necessary.
  b. Violence is justified—but only when all else fails.
  c. I am opposed to violence.
The figure given for 1971 represents the proportion who chose response "c."

TABLE 5   MARRIAGE AND FAMILY
(College Youth)

	1973 %	1971 %	1970 %	1969 %	1968 %
Feel that institution of marriage is becoming obsolete	32	34	28	24	*
Look forward to being legally married (based on those not yet married)	61	66	*	*	*
Interested in having children	76	79	*	*	*

*Question was not asked.

TABLE 6   BELIEF IN TRADITIONAL AMERICAN VALUES
(College Youth)

	1973 %	1971 %	1970 %	1969 %	1968 %
Business is entitled to make a profit	85	85	*	*	*
Doing any job well is important, no matter how menial	84	*	*	*	*
Commitment to a meaningful career is very important	81	79	*	*	*
People should save money regularly and not have to lean on family and friends the minute they run into financial problems	71	67	*	76	59
Private property is sacred	67	69	*	75	*
Depending on how much strength and character a person has, he can pretty well control what happens to him	65	60	*	62	51
Competition encourages excellence	62	62	*	72	*
Duty comes before pleasure	54	63	*	*	*
Hard work always pays off	44	39	*	56	69
People who accept things are better off than those who try to change them	15	*	*	*	*

*Question was not asked.

TABLE 7   SOCIAL RESTRAINTS THAT ARE EASILY ACCEPTABLE
(College Youth)

	1973 %	1971 %	1970 %	1969 %	1968 %
Prohibition against heroin	88	83	86	*	*
Prohibition against mind-expanding drugs	73	66	78	73	*
Power and authority of police	48	45	45	48	59
Power and authority of "boss" in a work situation	44	36	43	49	56
Prohibition against marijuana	38	42	48	48	55
Conformity in dress and personal appearance	33	33	39	33	37
Settling down to a routine	32	26	*	*	*
Outward conformity for sake of career/job	20	15	11	14	29
Abiding by laws you do not agree with	12	13	17	15	29

*Question was not asked.

TABLE 8   FUTURE CHANCES FOR SUCCESS
(College Youth)

	1973 %	1971 %	1970 %	1969 %	1968 %
Have no doubts about making as much money as desired	57	50	62	60	*
Have no doubts about being as successful as desired	76	64	*	67	*
See good opportunities to get ahead in the future	81	*	*	*	*

*Question was not asked.

TABLE 9   INFLUENCES ON JOB/CAREER CHOICE
(College Youth)

	1973 %	1971 %	1970 %	1969 %	1968 %
Challenge of the job	77	66	64	71	76
Opportunity to make a meaningful contribution	72	70	73	76	75
Free time for outside interests	69	59	*	*	*
Ability to express yourself	68	63	56	66	69
Money you can earn	61	44	36	41	41
Security	58	46	33	42	*
Chance to get ahead	51	35	*	*	*
Family	50	35	41	31	37
Prestige/status of the job	28	22	15	23	24

*Question was not asked.

TABLE 10   BARRIERS TO A DESIRABLE JOB
(College Youth)

	1973 %	1971 %
Attitudes toward authority	29	25
Unwillingness to conform	28	24
Educational background	27	17
Sex	24	16
Lack of vocational training	21	*
Race	14	11
Political views	13	15
Religion	7	5
Family background	7	6

*Question was not asked.

TABLE 11   REASONS WORTH FIGHTING A WAR FOR
(College Youth)

	1973 %	1971 %	1970 %	1969 %	1968 %
Counteracting aggression	50	50	50	56	64
Protecting our national interests	34	30	31	39	54
Protecting our allies	34	31	28	38	44
Containing communism	30	29	32	43	45
Maintaining a position of power	23	19	17	25	35
Fighting for our honor	19	18	17	25	33
Keeping a commitment	11	14	14	14	20

TABLE 12   RURAL AND COMMUNAL LIVING
(College Youth)

	1973 %	1971 %	1970 %	1969 %	1968 %
Interested in spending at least some time in a communal or collective living situation	30	36	*	*	*
Interested in spending at least some time in a rural or agricultural living situation	49	43	*	*	*

*Question was not asked.

TABLE 13   THE RADICAL DIAGNOSIS
(College Youth)

	1973 %	1971 %	1970 %	1969 %	1968 %
Believe this is a "sick" society	35	45	*	*	40
Believe this country is a democracy in name only and that special interests run things	63	57	*	*	*
Believe the American system is not flexible enough to solve its problems, or that it ought to be abolished	21	27	*	*	*

*Question was not asked.

TABLE 14   PERCEPTION OF POWER
(College Youth)

Where Real Power Vested*	1973 %	1971 %
Giant corporations	54	51
Congress	24	31
President	34	23
Financiers	30	26
General public	11	10
Special interest groups (i.e., labor, religious, etc.)	21	15
Defense department	14	21
CIA	5	10
Republican Party	4	3
Democratic Party	2	3

*Question was not asked prior to 1971.

TABLE 15   INSTITUTIONS THAT NEED FUNDAMENTAL REFORM OR ELIMINATION
(College Youth)

	1973 %	1971 %	1970 %	1969 %	1968 %
Penal system	69	61	69	*	*
Political parties	61	54	67	58	*
Military	54	67	72	61	*
Big business	54	46	50	38	*
High schools	52	*	50	*	*
Trade unions	38	39	48	43	*
FBI	37	39	31	*	*
Congress	34	34	38	*	*
Colleges/universities	31	36	43	32	*
Mass media	27	33	36	36	*
Supreme Court	21	24	33	*	*
Constitution	12	18	16	*	*

*Question was not asked.

TABLE 16   CRITICISM OF AMERICAN SOCIETY
(College Youth)

Those Who Agree Strongly or Partially	1973 %	1971 %	1970 %	1969 %	1968 %
Business is too concerned with profits and not with public responsibility	94	93	95	99	*
Our foreign policy is based on our own narrow economic and power interests	88	88	88	84	*
People's privacy is being destroyed	86	83	82	*	*
Basically we are a racist nation	79	81	89	78	*
We are rapidly losing our right to dissent	67	*	*	*	*
I am sick and tired of hearing people attack patriotism, morality, and other American values	65	*	*	*	*
There is more concern today for the welfare "bum" who doesn't want to work than for the hard working person who is struggling to make a living	64	68	*	69	*
Police should not hesitate to use force to maintain order	55	53	*	32	*
There is too much concern with equality and too little with law and order	53	49	*	57	*
The Establishment unfairly controls every aspect of our lives; we can never be free until we are rid of it	50	46	58	58	*
The country today pays too much attention to the needs of college students and not enough to the needs of young people who have to make a living	45	*	*	*	*

*Question was not asked.

TABLE 17 OPPRESSED GROUPS
(College Youth)

	1973 %	1971 %
American Indians	82	71
Homosexuals	82	84
Mexican-Americans	73	68
Blacks	71	81
Poor people	71	74
Old people	62	*
Women	58	33
Blue-collar workers	31	*
College students	26	27
Vietnam veterans	24	*
People whose parents were born in other countries	23	*

*Question was not asked.

TABLE 18 PARTY AFFILIATION AND VOTE CHOICE
(College Youth)

Party Identification	1973 %	1971 %	1970 %	1969 %	1968 %
Democrats	49	36	35	47	*
Republicans	24	21	22	25	*
None/other	27	43	43	28	*

*Question not asked or inappropriate.

TABLE 19 IDEOLOGICAL SELF-PERCEPTION
(College Youth)

	1973 %	1971 %	1970 %	1969 %	1968 %
Conservative and moderate/conservative	21	21	22	*	*
Moderate/middle-of-the-road and liberal/middle-of-the-road	52	44	47	*	*
Liberal and radical	27	35	31	*	*
Those Identifying with:					
New Left	9	11	14	13	13
The Movement	6	13	*	*	*

*Question was not asked.

TABLE 20 ALIENATION
(College Youth)

	1973 %	1971 %	1970 %	1969 %
Feel personal values are shared by most Americans	40	30	42	33
Anticipate no great difficulty in accepting the kind of life society has to offer	60	49	*	*

*Question was not asked.

DEMOGRAPHY

7

In almost all respects, college students and noncollege youth represent two distinctively different worlds in their socioeconomic backgrounds. These differences, plus the fact that one group is still in school while most of the other group is working full time or raising a family, probably account for many of the contrasting attitudes examined in later portions of this study.

Significant differences are found between the college and noncollege population in religion, race, parental income, parental education, father's occupation, and marital status:

A larger proportion of college students than noncollege youth profess no religious affiliation.

As might be expected, a disproportionately low number of nonwhites attend college.

Parents of noncollege youth have lower incomes and lower levels of education than college youth.

A majority of the fathers of noncollege youth are employed in blue-collar occupations, while a similar proportion of fathers of college students are in professional, executive, or managerial positions.

Noncollege young people are far more likely to be married and to have families than are college students.

At this point in their lives, noncollege youth tend to be at the bottom of the occupational and economic ladder, with the largest percentage involved in clerical work, Noncollege youth also contribute disproportionately to the ranks of the unemployed.

In the material that follows we summarize the important demographic characteristics of college and noncollege youth and then present the data in the form of a summary table.

FAMILY AND PERSONAL BACKGROUND

Age

By design, in order to include a representative sample of high school students, the noncollege sample has a larger number of sixteen- to ninteen-year-olds, while the college sample has more twenty- to twenty-one-year-olds.[1]

Religion

A much larger proportion of college students than noncollege youth claim no religious affiliation (16 percent to 9 percent). On the other hand, 78 percent of the noncollege group profess to be either Protestant or Catholic, while only 67 percent of the college students claim these religious ties. More than twice as many college students as noncollege youth are Jewish (7 percent to 3 percent).

Parents' Income

A majority of college students' parents have incomes in excess of $15,000 (51 percent), while only three out of ten (32 percent) parents of noncollege youth are in this income bracket. At the other end of the spectrum, nearly four out of ten parents of noncollege youth (39 percent) have incomes under $10,000 as compared with only two out of ten college students (23 percent).

---

[1]Although 30 percent of the noncollege sample consists of high school students, there are surprisingly few important attitudinal differences between them and the majority of noncollege youth. For this reason, we have grouped the two together. The major differences between these two noncollege subgroups are described in Chapter 15: *Noncollege Subgroups.*

Parents' Education

The parents of college students have considerably higher levels of education than the parents of noncollege youth: twice as many fathers and mothers of college students are college graduates. Among noncollege youth, four out of ten (39 percent) fathers did not graduate from high school, compared with only two out of ten (21 percent) fathers of college students. Similar differences can be seen in the educational level of mothers: 33 percent of mothers of noncollege youth are not high school graduates, while only 16 percent of the mothers of college youth failed to complete high school.

Father's Occupation

Consistent with the other findings in this section, a majority (51 percent) of the fathers of the noncollege group are blue-collar workers, with only 27 percent in professional, executive, or managerial positions. Almost the exact reverse is true for fathers of college students, with only 27 percent being in blue-collar occupations and 46 percent named as professionals, executives, or managers.

Marital Status

One out of three (30 percent) of the noncollege group are married (22 percent have children), whereas half that number of college students (15 percent) are married.

Union Membership

Almost equal proportions of the parents of the two groups (8 percent noncollege, 7 percent college) are union members. It is surprising that there is not a larger difference in the proportion of parents who come from union families, considering the much higher percentage of noncollege fathers who are blue-collar workers (51 percent to 27 percent).

Educational Background

Our noncollege sample reflects three levels of education: 43 percent had not completed high school, at least as of Spring 1973; an additional 32 percent were high school graduates; and 25 percent had some college education, although none were presently college students. Among high school graduates who did not go to college, approximately three out of ten took college preparatory courses in high school, while slightly more than half were enrolled in general programs. The remainder were in vocational or technical classes. Since leaving school (among those no longer enrolled) 28 percent have taken some additional courses or attended a school, either on the job or through their own initiative. (See Table 21—2*a-b*)

EMPLOYMENT

Employment Status

More than four out of ten noncollege youth (44 percent) are currently working more than twenty hours a week. An additional 20 percent work less than twenty hours a week. (Among those attending high school on a full-time basis, more than half are employed part time.) Slightly more than one out of ten are housewives (13 percent), or unemployed (11 percent). Among college youth, almost two out of three (62 percent) are employed at least part time. (See Table 21—3*a*)

Personal Income

More than six out of ten noncollege youth (62 percent) have personal incomes below $7,500. This, of course, includes a large number of people who work less than full time. College students working part time earn less. (See Table 21—3*b*)

Type of Occupation

Among those employed more than twenty hours per week, 27 percent are employed in clerical or technical jobs; 11 percent are in professional, executive, or managerial occupations, roughly an equal number, one out of ten, are craftsmen or operatives; less than one out of ten (6 percent) are laborers or engaged in skilled or unskilled services (6 percent). (See Table 21—3*c*)

TABLE 21   DEMOGRAPHY
By Total Noncollege Youth versus Total College Youth

	Total Noncollege %	Total College %
1. Two Worlds		
a. Age		
16-19 years	45	37
20-21 years	17	32
22-23 years	22	14
24 years and over	16	17

DEMOGRAPHY (Continued)

		Total Noncollege %	Total College %
b.	*Religion*		
	Protestant	45	40
	Catholic	33	27
	Jewish	3	7
	Other	10	10
	None	9	16
c.	*Race*		
	White	85	90
	Nonwhite	15	10
d.	*Parents' Income*		
	Under $7,500	22	10
	$7,500-9,999	17	13
	$10,000-14,999	29	26
	$15,000 and over	32	51
e.	*Father's Education*		
	Grade school	18	8
	Some high school	21	13
	High school graduate	31	28
	Some college	12	17
	College graduate or more	16	33
	Not sure	2	1
f.	*Mother's Education*		
	Grade school or less	13	5
	Some high school	20	11
	High school graduate	43	41
	Some college	12	20
	College graduate or more	10	21
	Not sure	2	2
g.	*Father's Occupation*		
	Professional/executive/managerial	27	46
	White-collar	16	15
	Blue-collar	51	27
	Other/retired/unemployed	6	12
h.	*Marital Status*		
	Single	67	84
	Married	30	15
	Widowed/divorced	3	1
	Have children	22	8
i.	*Union Membership*		
	Union member	8	7
	Union family	27	23
j.	*Vietnam Veterans*	7	7

DEMOGRAPHY (Continued)

		Total Noncollege %	Total College %
2.	**Educational Background**		
a.	*Education Completed*		
	8th grade or less	2	*
	1-2 years of high school	19	*
	3 years of high school	22	*
	Graduated high school	32	*
	1-2 years of college	14	*
	3 years of college	2	*
	College graduate	8	*
	Post-graduate	1	*
b.	*Type of High School Course†*		
	General	38	*
	College preparatory	21	*
	Vocational/technical	15	*
c.	*Courses Taken Since School*	28	*
3.	**Employment**		
a.	*Status*		
	Employed 35-40 hours per week } full	39	8
	Employed 20-34 hours per week } time	5	*
	Employed 10-19 hours per week } part	1	
	Employed less than 10 hours per week } time	1	54
	Full-time high school student	30	*
	Employed part time	18	*
	Not employed	12	*
	Housewife	13	*
	Unemployed	11	*
b.	*Personal Income‡*		
	Under $3,000	33	43
	$3,000-4,999	13	10
	$5,000-7,499	16	4
	$7,500-9,999	11	2
	$10,000-14,999	7	2
	$15,000 and over	2	1
c.	*Type of Occupation (Employed 20 hours or more)§*		
	Professional/executive/managerial	11	*

*Question was not asked.
†Asked of respondents who completed grade school but did not go to college.
‡Asked of respondents except nonworking high school and college students.
§Excluded employed high school students.

DEMOGRAPHY (Continued)

	Total Noncollege %	Total College %
Clerical/technical	27	*
Craftsmen	10	*
Operators	14	*
Laborers	6	*
Service-skilled	6	*
Service-unskilled	6	*
Armed services	2	*
Sales	4	*
All other	14	*

8

PERSONAL AND SOCIAL VALUES

The young people interviewed in this study, both college and noncollege, express considerable satisfaction with their lives. Both groups are highly optimistic about the future. But beneath the optimism, there are discernible differences in outlook and an undercurrent of discontent among the less educated youth.

Here are some of the survey's specific findings on young people's outlooks and self appraisals:

Personal Life.   A large majority of both college (78 percent) and noncollege (75 percent) youth say their lives are going well. Slightly more than eight out of ten (82 percent) noncollege youth are satisfied with their sex life, compared with three out of four (75 percent) college youth. In contrast, slightly more college than noncollege youth (71 percent compared with 66 percent) feel they are able to make ends meet financially. (See Table 22–1)

Quality of Education.   Approximately three out of ten (31 percent noncollege and 26 percent college) feel their past education was satisfactory for the kind of life they want to lead. Seventy percent of noncollege and 74 percent of college youth say they seek additional education. (See Table 22–2)

Self-Evaluation.   Roughly three-fourths of all young people say they enjoy their lives and are satisfied with themselves. A higher proportion of college students feel they are in control of their future (70 percent college to 63 percent noncollege) and have greater abilities than other people (47 percent college to 36 percent noncollege).

The absence of a college education is clearly correlated with feelings of insecurity and lack of self-confidence, with more noncollege youth feeling (a) trapped by lack of training, (b) left out of things, (c) discouraged about the future, and (d) convinced they will not be able to get ahead. (See Table 22–3)

Outlook for the Future.   Approximately two-thirds of all young people (66 percent college and 63 percent noncollege) say they have a clear idea of what they want to do in the future. Eighty-one percent of the college students feel they have good opportunities for the future, compared with 75 percent of noncollege youth. Similarly, more college than noncollege youth say they have no doubts about "making as much money as they want" (57 percent to 52 percent) or "being as successful as they want" (76 percent to 72 percent). (See Table 22–4)

TABLE 22   SELF-EVALUATION
By Total Noncollege Youth versus Total College Youth

	Total Noncollege %	Total College %
1. Personal Life		
Own life is going well	75	78
Sex life is satisfactory	82	75
Able to make ends meet	66	71

SELF-EVALUATION (Continued)

	Total Noncollege %	Total College %
2. Education		
Want more education	70	74
Have had poor education for kind of life I want	31	26
Family took it for granted I would go to college, not to work	57	72
Came from high school where most students go to college	49	63
3. Self-Evaluation		
I enjoy life very much	75	82
I'm satisfied with myself	72	75
I'm in control of my future	63	70
I'm more concerned with myself than with the world	39	51
I do things better than most people	36	47
I like to be independent but I can't	23	22
I feel uncomfortable with people with more education	19	17
I feel trapped by lack of training	18	15
I'm pretty discouraged about the future	18	13
I feel kind of left out of things	18	14
I just can't get ahead	16	9
I'm wasting time, not getting anywhere	16	11
I feel like a second-class citizen	15	11
I never got the guidance I needed	14	13
What I think doesn't count	13	10
I'm a political person	12	23
I rarely get a chance to enjoy myself	11	10
I find life pretty dull	10	6
4. Future		
Have a clear idea of what I want to do	63	66
Have good opportunities for future	75	81
Have no doubts about making as much money as I want	52	57
Have no doubts about being as successful as I want	72	76

NEW VALUES AND NONCOLLEGE YOUTH

Just four years ago there was a wide chasm between the moral and social outlook of college youth and the rest of the generation. Today this disparity no longer exists. Instead, the prevailing campus values of the late 1960s are now widely shared by noncollege youth. While it is true that during this same period college youth also intensified their commitment to the New Values, the striking fact today is not the contrast but the similarity in the present value structure and outlook of both campus and noncampus youth. Indeed, an entire generation of young people are now committed to the New Values, regardless of differences in their educational or socioeconomic backgrounds.

Details of the kinds of social changes noncollege youth now want and the impact of the New Values on their personal value outlook follow. (Work as a personal value and attitudes toward work are covered separately in Chapter 10.)

Social Changes Young People Would Welcome

The changes wanted in social values by the great mass of noncollege youth cover a wide range of subjects. Two of the most striking changes concern attitudes toward sex and money:

Among noncollege youth, 74 percent say they would now welcome less emphasis on money, compared with 54 percent in 1969.

Almost half (47 percent) of all noncollege youth would welcome more sexual freedom, compared with only 22 percent in 1969.

In addition, noncollege youth have lost some of their previous fervor for law and order and authority as social values:

A greater emphasis on law and order is now stressed by 68 percent, compared with 81 percent previously.

Sixty-six percent would welcome more respect for authority, compared with 86 percent in 1969. (See Tables 23–1 and 24–1)

Important Personal Values

Another sign of the adoption of the New Values by noncollege youth is the sharp decline in the importance they now attach to such traditional American values as patriotism, religion, and living a clean, moral life. Since 1969, the following changes have occurred:

Religion as a very important value is 42 percent now, compared to 65 percent in 1969.

Patriotism as a very important value is 40 percent now, compared to 61 percent in 1969.

Living a clean, moral life as a very important value is 57 percent now, compared to 78 percent in 1969.

Noncollege youth, however, continue to place far more stress than their college peers on the importance of doing things for others. Indeed, this has increased as a very important personal value among noncollege youth from the 55 percent level in 1969 to 64 percent this year. (See Tables 23–2 and 24–2)

Decline in Traditional American Beliefs

While a large majority of American young people who do not attend college continue to believe in most aspects of the puritan ethic, some erosion has occurred, with fewer young people now believing in thrift (80 percent now, 89 percent in 1969); the sacredness of private property (74 percent now, 88 percent previously); hard work always paying off (56 percent now, 79 percent previously); and competition encouraging excellence (66 percent now, 81 percent previously). (See Tables 23–5 and 24–3)

Moral Codes

In many ways, the one theme of the New Values that has enjoyed the greatest influence among the noncollege youth is the belief in a freer, more open attitude toward sex. Four years ago, a majority of noncollege youth (in contrast to the prevailing view on campus) considered the following activities to be morally wrong: abortion (63 percent), relations between consenting homosexuals (72 percent), casual premarital sexual relations (58 percent), and extramarital sexual relations (78 percent).

Today, the noncollege youth population feels differently about these same issues, with only extramarital relations continuing to be regarded as a moral question by a majority. Homosexuality, for example, is now considered to be morally wrong by only 47 percent of the noncollege youth. Aside from sexual morality, the general moral code of the noncollege young people is still somewhat stricter than the prevailing norms of the campus. Activities considered to be morally wrong by a majority of noncollege youth include:

Destroying private property (88 percent).

Paying for college by selling dope (80 percent).

Cheating big companies (66 percent).

Having children without formal marriage (58 percent).
(See Tables 23—6 and 24—4)

Attitudes About Marriage

The views of noncollege youth toward marriage are somewhat more ambivalent than the comparable attitudes of college youth. On the one hand, noncollege youth look forward to the idea of getting married somewhat less than do college youth (48 percent to 53 percent). Yet when marriage is an accomplished fact, they take a sterner view than do college students about the immorality of extramarital relations (65 percent noncollege, 60 percent college). They are also stronger in their opposition to swapping partners among couples. Among noncollege youth, 72 percent consider "swapping" to be morally wrong, compared with 57 percent among college youth. (Table 23—3-6)

Having Children

Three out of four college and noncollege youth look forward to having children—but their feelings about the subject are somewhat different. A larger proportion of noncollege young people regard having children as an important life value (45 percent), as compared with 31 percent of the campus youth who attach the same importance to this commitment. In addition, noncollege youth strike a much firmer opposition to the idea of planning and having a family without formal marriage. Among noncollege youth, 58 percent consider this to be morally wrong; among college youth, only 40 percent feel the same way. (Table 23—4 & 6)

Family

Noncollege youth place considerably more emphasis than college students on the importance of family as a personal value (noncollege 81 percent, college 68 percent). (Table 23—2)

Changing Attitudes Toward War as National Policy

The Vietnam War and the New Values on campus have combined to leave a permanent mark on the views of American young people regarding war as an instrument of national policy.

Four years ago, in 1969, six out of ten high school students, members of the working class, the unemployed, and other young people under the age of 25 felt that it was worthwhile to fight a war to counteract agression (67 percent), contain communism (69 percent), protect our national interests (66 percent), and fight for our honor (59 percent). At least half felt it was also worthwhile to fight a war to protect our allies or maintain our position of power in the world. Today, only one out of two of noncollege youth consider counteracting aggression (53 percent), containing communism (50 percent), or protecting our national interests (49 percent) as worthy reasons for fighting a war, turning down all other motivations, including protecting our allies (46 percent), fighting for our honor (43 percent), or maintaining our position of power in the world (40 percent). The two largest differences between the viewpoints of noncollege and college youth are in their attitudes toward wars to contain communism (noncollege 50 percent, college 30 percent) and fighting for our honor (noncollege 43 percent, college 19 percent). (Tables 23–7 and 24–5)

Drugs

Only one out of two noncollege youth are able to accept easily the present restraints against marijuana, a sharp decline from the 71 percent who easily accepted the prohibition in 1969. Yet, neither college students nor noncollege youth have any difficulty in accepting the restraints against mind-expanding drugs or heroin. (Tables 23–8 and 24–6)

Conformity and Authority

Today's noncollege youth have greater difficulty in accepting authority—either from the boss in a work situation or from the police—than their peers did in 1969. Curiously, while college students' views have mellowed in this respect, the views of the noncollege majority have not. Today, noncollege youth accept less easily the power of the boss in a work situation (57 percent now, 71 percent in 1969) and the power and authority of the police (60 percent now, 79 percent in 1969).

In terms of social conformity, the picture is somewhat different. More than one out of three noncollege youth continue to be willing to conform outwardly for the sake of a career or job advancement (37 percent now, 35 percent in 1969). They are less willing now, however, to conform in matters of dress and personal grooming (42 percent now, 54 percent in 1969). In this case, too, college youth take the same stand that they did in 1969—with one out of three (33 percent) willing to concede to social norms, at least in matters of personal appearance.

Life Style

Noncollege youth are somewhat readier to accept a conventional life style, like that of their parents, than are college students (noncollege 75 percent, college 68 percent). Also, college students are more interested in experimenting with alternative life styles, such as living in a commune (28 percent college, 21 percent noncollege) or living in an agricultural community (42 percent and 32 percent respectively). (Table 23–9)

TABLE 23   PERSONAL AND SOCIAL VALUES
By Total Noncollege Youth versus Total College Youth

	Total Noncollege %	Total College %
1. Welcome Social Changes		
More emphasis on self-expression	76	83
Less emphasis on money	74	80
More emphasis on law and order	68	51
More respect for authority	66	48
More emphasis on technological improvements	61	55
More emphasis on traditional family ties	61	51
More acceptance of sexual freedom	47	61
Less emphasis on working hard	35	31
Less emphasis on permissiveness	33	33
More acceptance of drug usage	15	19
2. Very Important Personal Values		
Love	88	87
Friendship	87	86
Fulfilling yourself as a person	87	87
Family	81	68
Privacy	78	71
Education	75	76
Doing things for others	64	56
Living a clean and moral life	57	34
Work	53	43
Being creative	52	50
Being close to nature	50	45
Having children	45	31
Religion	42	23
Patriotism	40	19
Money	34	20
Changing society	27	24

PERSONAL AND SOCIAL VALUES (Continued)

	Total Noncollege %	Total College %
3. Attitudes Toward Marriage		
Disagree that marriage is becoming obsolete	62	67
Look forward to being legally married	48	53
4. Children		
Interested in having children	78	76
5. Belief in Traditional American Values		
Doing any job well is important	89	84
Business is entitled to make a profit	85	85
People should save money regularly	80	71
Commitment to a meaningful career is very important	79	81
Private property is sacred	74	67
A "strong" person can control own life	70	65
Competition encourages excellence	66	62
Duty comes before pleasure	66	54
Hard work will always pay off	56	44
Man is basically good, but society corrupts	50	46
People who accept things are better off	31	15
6. Activities Thought to Be Morally Wrong		
Destroying private property	88	78
Taking things without paying for them	88	84
Collecting welfare when you could work	83	77
Paying for college by selling dope	80	64
Interchanging partners among couples	72	57
Using violence to achieve worthwhile results	72	66
Cheating big companies	66	50
Extramarital sexual relations	65	60
Having children without formal marriage	58	40
Living with a spouse you do not love	52	41
Having an abortion	48	32
Relations between consenting homosexuals	47	25
Casual premarital sexual relations	34	22
7. Reasons Worth Fighting a War for		
Counteracting aggression	53	50
Containing communism	50	30
Protecting our national interest	49	34

PERSONAL AND SOCIAL VALUES (Continued)

	Total Noncollege %	Total College %
Protecting our allies	46	34
Fighting for our honor	43	19
Maintaining our position of power in the world	40	23
Keeping a commitment	23	11

8. **Restraints Willingly and Easily Accepted**

Prohibition against heroin	80	88
Prohibition against mind-expanding drugs	71	73
Power and authority of the police	60	48
Power and authority of the "boss" in a work situation	57	44
Prohibition against marijuana	49	38
Settling down to a routine	47	32
Conformity in matters of dress and personal grooming	42	33
Outward conformity for the sake of career or job advancement	37	20
Abiding by laws you do not agree with	24	12

9. **Life Style**

   a. Conventional Life Style

Same kind of life as my parents	12	8
No difficulty in accepting kind of life society has to offer	63	60
Not going to be easy to accept conventional life—no alternatives	12	17
Conventional life intolerable	12	13
Not sure	1	2

   b. Alternative Life Styles

Interested in living in a commune		
Short term	21	28
Permanent	2	2
Interested in living off land or in small agricultural community		
Short term	32	42
Permanent	9	7

TABLE 24 PERSONAL AND SOCIAL VALUES
Trend Data

	Noncollege		College	
	1973 %	1969 %	1973 %	1969 %
1. Welcome Social Changes				
More emphasis on self-expression	76	70	83	84
Less emphasis on money	74	54	80	72
More emphasis on law and order	68	81	51	58
More respect for authority	66	86	48	59
More emphasis on technological improvements	61	64	55	56
More acceptance of sexual freedom	47	22	61	43
Less emphasis on working hard	35	32	31	24
2. Very Important Personal Values				
Love	88	90	87	85
Friendship	87	90	86	84
Privacy	78	74	71	62
Education	75	81	76	80
Doing things for others	64	55	56	51
Living a clean, moral life	57	78	34	46
Religion	42	65	28	39
Patriotism	40	61	19	35
Money	34	40	20	18
Changing society	27	29	24	33
3. Belief in Traditional American Values				
People should save money regularly	80	89	71	76
Private property is sacred	74	88	67	76
A "strong" person can control own life	70	77	65	62
Competition encourages excellence	66	81	62	72
Hard work will always pay off	56	79	44	57
4. Activities Thought to Be Morally Wrong				
Extramarital sexual relations	65	78	60	77
Having an abortion	48	63	32	36
Relations between consenting homosexuals	47	72	25	42
Casual premarital sexual relations	34	58	22	34

PERSONAL AND SOCIAL VALUES (Continued)

	Noncollege		College	
	1973 %	1969 %	1973 %	1969 %
5. Reasons Worth Fighting a War for				
Counteracting aggression	53	67	50	57
Containing communism	50	69	30	43
Protecting own national interest	49	66	34	38
Protecting our allies	46	50	34	38
Fighting for our honor	43	59	19	25
Maintaining our position of power in world	40	51	23	25
Keeping a commitment	23	28	11	14
6. Restraints Willingly and Easily Accepted				
Prohibition against mind-expanding drugs†	71	79	73	73
Power and authority of the police	60	79	48	48
Power and authority of the "boss" in a work situation	57	71	44	49
Prohibition against marijuana	49	71	38	49
Conformity in matters of dress and personal grooming	42	54	33	33
Outward conformity for the sake of career or job advancement	37	35	20	14
Abiding by laws you do not agree with	24	34	12	15

†Asked about "LSD" in 1960. Asked about "mind-expanding drugs" in 1973.

9

WOMEN'S LIBERATION AND WOMEN

The Women's Movement has made a decided impact on the views of America's young people. This chapter looks first at the different—and sometimes similar—influence Women's Liberation has had on noncollege youth compared to college youth. Then it looks at the significant difference the survey finds between college and noncollege women themselves, including differences over Women's Liberation itself.

WOMEN'S LIBERATION

Unlike most of the recent political and social movements of the 1950s and the 1960s, the initial impetus for the Women's Movement had little to do with the college campus. This has not, however, diminished campus support for many of the beliefs and principles advanced by the Women's Movement. Campus readiness and responsiveness is indicated in a number of different ways.

The campus view of women as an oppressed group has almost doubled in the last two years, with well over half of the students now sharing in this opinion.

A large majority of the students on campus accept the concepts of male-female equality in sexual relations, sisterhood and the importance of women's relations to other women, and the idea that men and women are born with the same basic nature and talents.

Noncollege youth, too, have been influenced by the thrust of the Women's Movement—but they clearly find it harder to integrate some of the ideas of the movement with their own more traditional views of male-female relations and their own economic concerns. For example, noncollege students are less ready than college students to accept the concepts of sisterhood or to consider women as an exploited sector of society. On the other hand, noncollege students as a group are also:

Solidly behind equal pay for equal work.

Prepared to believe that it is as important for a "real man" to be concerned about the sexual satisfaction of his partner as it is for him to be a good provider and "family man."

No longer committed to the idea that the man must be the main decision maker in the family.

Ready to accept the idea that women should be as free as men to take the initiative in sex.

Here are some of the specific findings:

Definition of a Real Man. Compared to the college students, the definition of a "real man" in the eyes of the noncollege youth is a curious blend of traditional American views and the impact of the Women's Movement.

The traditional side of noncollege youth is represented by the 77 percent who identify the key attributes of a "real man" with being a good provider and holding strong views about what is right and wrong. The impact of the Women's Movement can be seen in the comparable percentage (75 percent) who emphasize concern with a woman's sexual satisfaction.

College students, advancing beyond this point, now place far greater emphasis on concern with a woman's sexual satisfaction (77 percent) than with being a good provider (56 percent). (See Table 25–1)

Agreement with Women's Liberation Arguments.   Noncollege young people are far less ready to regard women as a discriminated group than their college peers. This does not stop them, however, from overwhelming endorsement of equal pay for equal work (91 percent) or from proclaiming surprising support for many of the more controversial concepts of Women's Liberation:

The idea that "woman's place is in the home" is nonsense (47 percent).

Women are as logical as men (49 percent).

Men and women are born with the same human nature; "it's the way they are brought up that makes them different" (56 percent).

Noncollege young adults are somewhat less sympathetic than college students to the notion that the relationship of women to women is just as important as women's relationship to men (47 percent noncollege, 64 percent college), or to the idea that "there is almost no job that a man can do that a woman can't do just as well" (28 percent noncollege, 36 percent college). Together with college students, they reject in large numbers the more extreme ideas of Women's Liberation:

The belief that taking care of a home and raising children is not as fulfilling for a woman as having a job or a career is supported by 22 percent noncollege youth and 18 percent college students.

The view that a woman has the right to put her own fulfillment ahead of her obligations to her husband and children finds a very low level of support (noncollege 19 percent, college 19 percent). (Table 25–2)

TABLE 25   WOMEN'S LIBERATION
By Total Noncollege Youth versus Total College Youth

	Total Noncollege %	Total College %
1. Very Important Qualities in a Man		
Good provider	77	56
Has strong views about what is right/wrong	76	57
Concern with a woman's sexual satisfaction	75	77
Puts family above everything else	67	48
Shows women courtesy and respect	63	45
Able to satisfy a woman sexually	60	53
Keeps feelings under control	48	30
Cannot be pushed around by women	40	32
Makes the decisions in the family	40	20
Treats men and women exactly the same	32	29
Handy around the house	31	17
Willing to do household chores	30	35
Physically strong	27	15
Good looking in a masculine way	16	12
2. Agreement with Women's Liberation Arguments		
Women should receive equal pay with men for equal work	91	95
Women should be as free as men to take the initiative in sex relations	70	84
Men and women are born with the same human nature; it's the way they are brought up that makes them different	56	57
The idea that women are more emotional and less logical than men is ridiculous	49	53
The idea that a woman's place is in the home is nonsense	47	57
The relationship of a woman to other women is just as important as a woman's relationship to men	47	64
A woman does not have to have a man around to be happy	42	49
There is almost no job that a man can do that a woman cannot do just as well	28	36
Taking care of a home and raising children is not as fulfilling for a woman as having a job or a career	22	18
A woman has the right to put her own self-fulfillment ahead of her obligations to her husband and children	19	19

COLLEGE VERSUS NONCOLLEGE WOMEN

One finding of the youth generation research that may have particularly important implications for the future is that a sharp cleavage in views and values now separates college and noncollege women.

College women have become the champion of many of the causes of Women's Liberation, the leaders in the crusade for self-fulfillment as a basic right for women as well as men. On almost every front they are challenging traditional concepts of the woman's role—as helper, homemaker, and passive sexual partner—and in the process they are inadvertently pulling many of the social underpinnings out from under young women who work because they need the money or who feel that their value in society is based on being good wives and mothers.

The polarization between the two groups of women is further accentuated by the fact that both college and noncollege men tend to take less extreme positions than their female counterparts.

Contrasts between the two groups of women are apparent in a number of areas.

Discrimination

Noncollege women are, by far, less convinced than college women that women as a group are treated unfairly (noncollege women 41 percent, college women 63 percent).

Values

Wide differences exist in the value structure of noncollege and college women.

Noncollege women say they have a strong commitment to living a clean, moral life (62 percent); college women do not share the same commitment (39 percent).

Noncollege women are considerably less ready to welcome more acceptance of sexual freedom (38 percent) than college women (59 percent).

Having children is an important personal value to 50 percent of the noncollege women and to only 31 percent of the college women.

Almost two-thirds of the noncollege women (62 percent) regard having children outside of formal marriage as morally wrong. This view is shared by only 40 percent of the college women.

While the differences are great, it would be wrong to assume that non-college women have not been influenced by the New Values. Only a minority (41 percent), for example, now look upon casual premarital sexual relations as morally wrong. (Table 26—1)

Definition of a Real Man

Noncollege women cling to the more traditional definition of masculinity, yet they also introduce an important new component into the definition. In addition to the concept of a man as a good provider, noncollege women are also stressing the importance of man's concern with a woman's sexual satisfaction.

Noncollege and college women say that a real man should:

Be a good provider (noncollege women 79 percent, college women 56 percent).

Hold strong views about what is right and wrong (noncollege women 76 percent, college women 61 percent).

Be concerned with a woman's sexual satisfaction (noncollege women 78 percent, college women 80 percent).

Put family above everything else (noncollege women 70 percent, college women 46 percent).

Show women courtesy and respect (noncollege women 66 percent, college women 45 percent). (Table 26—2)

Women's Liberation

While less enthusiastic than their college sisters, a majority of noncollege women accept some of the mainstream arguments of the Women's Movement about the fundamental equality of men and women:

Men and women are born with the same human nature; it's the way that they are brought up that makes them different (noncollege women 55 percent, college women 61 percent).

Women are as logical as men (noncollege women 50 percent, college women 59 percent).

But the groups diverge over the role of women and over the importance of sisterhood:

Woman's place is *not* in the home (noncollege women 47 percent, college women 64 percent).

Women should be as free as men to take the initiative in sex relations (noncollege women 67 percent, college women 83 percent).

The relationship of women to other women is just as important as women's relationship to men (noncollege women 49 percent, college women 67 percent). (Table 26–3)

TABLE 26   VIEWS OF WOMEN'S LIBERATION
By Total Noncollege Women versus Total College Women

	Noncollege Women %	College Women %
1. Sex and Morality		
a. Very Important Personal Values		
Love	91	93
Friendship	86	88
Living a clean, moral life	62	39
Having children	50	35
b. Would Welcome More Acceptance of Sexual Freedom	38	59
c. Activities Thought to Be Morally Wrong		
Interchanging partners among couples	79	64
Extramarital sexual relations	71	65
Living with a spouse you do not love	53	43
Having children without formal marriage	62	41
Having an abortion	52	38
Relations between consenting homosexuals	48	24
Casual premarital sexual relations	41	29
d. Attitudes Toward Marriage		
Disagree that marriage is becoming obsolete	66	69
Look forward to being legally married	51	62
e. Interest in Having Children	83	77
2. Very Important Qualities in a Man		
Good provider	79	56
Has strong views about what is right/wrong	76	61
Concern with a woman's sexual satisfaction	78	80
Puts family above everything else	70	46

WOMEN'S LIBERATION (Continued)

	Noncollege Women %	College Women %
Shows women courtesy and respect	66	45
Able to satisfy a woman sexually	61	60
Keeps feelings under control	43	24
Cannot be pushed around by women	41	33
Makes the decisions in the family	36	19
Treats men and women exactly the same	33	28
Handy around the house	29	17
Willing to do household chores	29	35
Physically strong	26	18
Good looking in a masculine way	16	16

3. **Agreement with Women's Liberation Arguments**

	Noncollege Women %	College Women %
Women should receive equal pay with men for equal work	94	98
Women should be as free as men to take the initiative in sex relations	67	83
Men and women are born with the same human nature; it's the way they are brought up that makes them different	55	61
The idea that women are more emotional and less logical than men is ridiculous	50	59
The idea that a woman's place is in the home is nonsense	47	64
The relationship of a woman to other women is just as important as a woman's realtionship to men	49	67
A woman does not have to have a man around to be happy	43	49
There is almost no job that a man can do that a woman cannot do just as well	31	39
Taking care of a home and raising children is not as fulfilling for a woman as having a job or a career	19	16
A woman has the right to put her own self-fulfillment ahead of her obligations to her husband and children	18	18

10
WORK AND CAREER

It is with respect to work and career that the real differences between having and not having a college education show up most vividly. The major differences are not in goals or priorities, but rather in what happens to the young high school graduate compared to the college-trained professional when they enter the work force.

Both groups clearly are searching for the same objective—a job that is not "just a job," but an opportunity to use one's capabilities and do interesting work. Nor are there large differences in their expressed priorities. Among college students, a majority (57 percent) claim that they now take economic security for granted and will make self-realization their prime career target for the future. A substantial minority of noncollege youth (43 percent) express this same orientation.

One of the subgroups in our sample is composed of the young managerial and professional men and women who have recently graduated from college and professional schools and are now enjoying the fruits of their years of training. These well-educated young people, almost from the start of their careers, are finding the kinds of satisfaction from work they so eagerly seek, while the noncollege youth are finding essentially dull and personally unrewarding jobs, as indicated by these findings:

Blue-collar workers are less satisfied with their present jobs than either young white-collar, professional, or managerial young people.

Only one out of three blue-collar workers feels that there is a future in his or her job.

Blue-collar workers recognize lack of education as their main career barrier.

There is real eagerness among young workers for more training. They state that they are ready to take a pay cut in order to acquire it.

JOB CRITERIA

Despite some difference in future outlook, there are remarkably few differences in the job criteria of blue-collar, white-collar, and college-trained, professional young people. While blue-collar workers as a group place greater emphasis on good pay (blue-collar 65 percent, white-collar 60 percent, professional/executive 53 percent), they are only slightly less committed to meaningful and interesting work than other young workers.

The top job criteria for the majority of all young working people include:

Friendly, helpful co-workers (70 percent).

Work that is interesting (70 percent).

Opportunity to use your mind (65 percent).

Work results you can see (62 percent).

Pay that is good (61 percent).

Opportunity to develop skills/abilities (61 percent).

Participation in decisions regarding job (58 percent).

Getting help needed to do the job well (55 percent).

Respect for organization you work for (55 percent).

Recognition for a job well done (54 percent).

(See Table 27—2)

How Present Jobs Meet the Criteria

The levels of satisfaction that young people attribute to their present jobs show clear-cut differences between college-educated and noncollege young people:

Fifty-nine percent of the college-trained professional and executive youth find their work interesting; only 43 percent of the blue-collar youth feel the same way about their jobs.

Sixty-two percent of those in professional and executive jobs report they have a chance to use their minds at work; only 38 percent of the blue-collar workers feel the same.

Fifty-seven percent of the better-educated young people feel they have a chance to develop their skills and abilities, compared to 33 percent of the young blue-collar workers.

Still, the vast majority of young working people (73 percent) say they would continue to work even if they had enough money to live comfortably without working. (Table 27—4-5)

Readiness for Education and Training

One out of two (48 percent) blue-collar workers mention lack of education as the major barrier they face in getting the kinds of jobs they desire.

Sixty-eight percent of the young blue-collar workers and 65 percent of the white-collar workers report they would be willing to take a 20 percent pay cut in order to take advantage of a six-month training program (sponsored by employer, government, or union, etc.) which might lead to a promotion or a better job. (Table 27—5)

TABLE 27   WORK AND CAREER
By Total Noncollege Youth versus Total College Youth

	Total Noncollege %	Total College %
1. Future Priorities		
Economic security and providing for my family comes first	57	43
I'm not that concerned with economic security. I guess I take it for granted. I'm more concerned with doing things that will give me a sense of self-fulfillment	43	57

WORK AND CAREER (Continued)
By Noncollege Youth Employed 20 Hours or More Per Week*

	Total Employed 20 Hours or More %	Blue-Collar %	White-Collar %	Professional, Executive, Managerial %
2. Things Wanted in a Job				
Friendly co-workers	70	68	76	67
Interesting work	70	66	76	78
Chance to use your mind	65	58	71	80
Work results you can see	62	60	63	71
Chance to develop skills and abilities	61	57	58	80
Good pay	61	65	60	53
Participation in decisions regarding job	58	56	63	63
Good chances for promotion	55	51	61	56
Respect for the organization you work for	55	52	59	59
Help available to do the job well	55	54	61	48
Recognition for a job well done	54	52	58	57
Person in charge who is concerned about you	53	52	57	55
Good job security	52	50	55	55
Opportunities to talk up without getting into trouble	51	50	53	52
Chance to work at a variety of things	48	48	47	53
Really competent person in charge	47	46	47	59
Clearly defined responsibilities	47	44	56	37
Enough time to do job well	47	48	50	39
Good fringe benefits	47	45	55	41
Conformity in dress/politics not required	45	48	47	34
Freedom to decide how to do your work	43	41	40	58

*44% of total noncollege youth.

WORK AND CAREER (Continued)

	Total Employed 20 Hours or More %	Blue- Collar %	White- Collar %	Profes- sional, Executive, Managerial %
Time for outside interest	43	45	45	34
As much responsibility as you can handle	42	37	43	56
No one standing over you/ being own boss	41	40	42	41
Regular raises whether promoted or not	41	42	41	39
Job not just anyone can fill	39	38	37	48
Work that is socially useful	38	35	44	40
Job in growing field/industry	38	39	40	36
Not being caught up in a big impersonal organization	38	34	41	46
Chance to make a lot of money later on	37	39	37	30
Good pension plan and early retirement	37	39	36	34
Formal on-the-job training courses	30	28	34	32
Job that is not too demand- ing	26	26	27	22
Job that doesn't involve hard physical work	23	18	33	25
Not being expected to do things not paid for	21	24	18	19

3. General Job Satisfaction

   a. *Level of Satisfaction with Job*

Very satisfied	38	34	42	47
Somewhat satisfied	41	44	36	38
Not too satisfied	13	15	11	12
Not at all satisfied	5	6	6	—
Not sure	3	1	5	3

   b. *Sources of Satisfaction*

My family	39	38	38	47
Personal relationships outside family	27	29	27	20
Interest, activities, out- side the job	27	26	30	24

WORK AND CAREER (Continued)

	Total Employed 20 Hours or More %	Blue-Collar %	White-Collar %	Profes-sional, Executive, Managerial %
My job	5	4	3	8
Not sure	2	3	2	1
c. *Relationship to Job*				
I work hard, but I'm not married to the job	48	54	51	27
My job is more than just a job	27	23	24	47
I'd work harder if I got recognition	17	14	19	21
I'm not getting a fair deal on the job	6	8	5	2
Not sure	2	1	1	3
d. *If Had to Decide All Over Again*				
Take same job without hesitation	66	62	68	73
Have some second thoughts	24	27	22	20
Decide definitely not to take job	10	11	10	7
e. *Feelings About Job*				
I like the people I work with	61	57	67	66
I take pride in my job and do it well	52	50	51	67
It's a job with a future	35	30	34	57
I want more training—to do something else	28	32	25	20
I can live with what I have	24	28	21	16
I'm just hanging on till something better shows up	24	31	20	11
I look forward to going to work each day	22	18	25	29
It's a chance to make a living	18	23	15	10

WORK AND CAREER (Continued)

	Total Employed 20 Hours or More %	Blue- Collar %	White- Collar %	Profes- sional, Executive, Managerial %
I don't expect much from a job	11	12	12	7
I'm stuck in a dead end	9	8	10	8
I don't like it, but I have no other choice	8	11	5	3

4. Specific Sources of Satisfaction with Present Job

	Total Employed 20 Hours or More %	Blue- Collar %	White- Collar %	Profes- sional, Executive, Managerial %
Friendly co-workers	62	61	65	62
Good pay	61	65	60	53
Work results you can see	51	50	50	56
Interesting work	48	43	54	59
Chance to use your mind	45	38	48	62
Conformity in dress/politics not required	33	39	30	20
Respect for the organization you work for	44	42	49	43
Good job security	41	37	45	46
Help available to do the job well	37	37	43	28
Chance to develop skills and abilities	37	33	33	57
Person in charge who is concerned about you	37	36	40	36
Chance to work at a variety of things	37	35	38	40
Recognition for a job well done	36	35	39	37
Opportunities to talk up without getting into trouble	35	35	34	37
Clearly defined responsibilities	34	34	42	22
Enough time to do job well	34	34	38	30
Good fringe benefits	34	30	42	35
Participation in decisions regarding job	34	31	39	40

WORK AND CAREER (Continued)

	Total Employed 20 Hours or More %	Blue-Collar %	White-Collar %	Professional, Executive, Managerial %
Time for outside interests	33	33	36	24
Good chance for promotion	31	27	35	40
Job in growing field/industry	29	29	30	31
Work that is socially useful	28	24	29	35
Freedom to decide how to do your work	28	25	26	41
Job not just anyone can fill	27	24	27	40
Not being caught up in big impersonal organization	27	24	28	38
No one standing over you/ being own boss	27	26	27	31
As much responsibility as you can handle	26	23	26	35
Regular raises whether promoted or not	24	25	24	23
Really competent person in charge	22	22	23	21
Good pension plan and early retirement	21	21	21	23
Chance to make a lot of money later on	20	20	17	24
Job that doesn't involve hard physical work	18	13	26	20
Job that is not too demanding	17	18	19	12
Formal on-the-job training courses	16	13	18	20
Not being expected to do things not paid for	14	18	10	13
5. Interest in Work/Training				
Would work even if had enough money to live comfortably	73	73	71	82
Would take six-month training program leading to promotion or better job even at 20% pay cut	66	68	65	61

11
ALTERNATIVE OPTIONS

When young people leave high school, few of them see any options other than starting to work full time or continuing their education in college. This does not mean, however, that they would not be interested in alternative options if these were made available. Indeed, there appears to be a genuine desire for a wider spectrum of choices, not only among noncollege youth, but also among those who went on to college.

Among those now attending college, social pressures seemed to have played an important role in their decision to go to college. Unlike many other Americans, the majority of college students were almost predestined to go to college after graduation from high school because three out of four (72 percent) came from families where it was "always taken for granted" that they would go on to college; two out of three attended high schools where most of the students went on to college (63 percent); and three out of four (72 percent) felt that they had no option when they graduated high school other than to go to college or take a job.

Given this background, one of the more interesting findings of this study is the interest college students show in a series of alternative options, had they been available when they graduated from high school.

FIVE OPTIONS

Respondents in both the college and noncollege samples were asked to evaluate how interested they might be in each of five alternative plans that could be offered upon leaving high school.

A Start-Your-Own-Business Program featuring training and interest-free loans.

New Types of Technical Schools offering certified training for skills needed in expanding industries.

A Career-Planning Year exposing the person to many different fields and job opportunities and featuring career counseling.

New Types of Apprenticeship Programs in industry, the arts, unions, or service organizations, where the person is paid minimum wages while he learns high-paying skills.

A Six-Year Job-and-College Program where the person works steadily at the job and gets a college degree for both work and formal courses taken at a nearby college.

These five plans drew great interest from *both* college and noncollege young people. In both groups, the two most popular options were the Career-Planning Year and the Six-Year Job-and-College Program.

Asked to pick the single plan in which they might be most interested, both groups put the Six-Year Job-and-College Program on top by a wide margin—clearly indicating that those not in college still see education as a vital ingredient to future success.

Now for the specifics.

Alternatives After High School

Only a minority of either college (28 percent) or noncollege (37 percent) young adults perceive any realistic options after high school other than taking a job or going on to college. The wider sense of choice expressed by those not in college comes mainly from the women in this group for whom the prospects of becoming a homemaker hold greater attraction than the job/education alternatives. The other major alternatives are the military and vocational training—each mentioned by about one in ten of each group. (See Table 28—1)

Interest in Option Plans

When our respondents were presented with the series of five alternative options, they were first asked to indicate which of the plans interested them. The levels of interest expressed were as follows:

Career-Planning Year: 75 percent noncollege, 80 percent college.

Six-Year College-and-Work Plan: 71 percent noncollege, 82 percent college.

New Apprenticeship Programs: 63 percent noncollege, 60 percent college.

Certified Technical Training: 59 percent noncollege, 47 percent college.

Start-Your-Own-Business Program: 45 percent noncollege, 44 percent college.

Respondents were then asked to indicate which *one* of these plans they might be *most* interested in. The Six-Year College-and-Work Plan was the favorite among both groups, though more so for the college (48 percent) than the noncollege group (31 percent). Next in line came the Career-Planning Year, with endorsements by one out of four in both groups. The noncollege young people gave relatively greater support to the other three plans:

Start-Your-Own-Business Program: (16 Percent to 10 percent).

New Apprenticeship Programs: (11 percent to 7 percent).

Certified Technical Training: (10 percent to 3 percent).

(See Table 28—2-3)

Confidence in High School Counselors

Noncollege youth were also asked how much confidence they might have in the advice of a high school counselor to help clear up doubts about which of the option plans would be most suitable for them. Only a few (15 percent) stated that they would have a great deal of confidence, while about half (48 percent) felt they would have at least some confidence. Another 25 percent expressed no real confidence at all in the advice of a high school counselor. (See Table 28—4)

TABLE 28   ALTERNATIVE OPTIONS
By Total Noncollege Youth Versus Total College Youth

		Total Noncollege %	Total College %
1.	**Availability of Alternative Options**		
	a. *Had Other Alternatives After Graduating High School†*	37	28
	b. *Choices Available*		
	Military service	12	13
	Becoming a homemaker	10	4
	Vocational/trade school	9	7
	Going to business school	5	4
	On-the-job training	4	3
	Studying arts/music	3	2
	Other	6	7
	Not sure	2	—
2.	**Options Would Seriously Consider**		
	#3: Career-planning year	75	80
	#5: Six-year college-and-work plan	71	82
	#4: New type apprentice program	63	60
	#2: Certified technical training	59	47
	#1: Start-your-own-business program	45	44
3.	**Option with the Most Interest**		
	#5: Six-year college-and-work plan	31	48
	#3: Career-planning year	24	26
	#1: Start-your-own-business program	16	10
	#4: New type apprentice program	11	7
	#2: Certified technical training	10	3
	None/not sure	8	6
4.	**Advice from High School Counselor in Making a Decision**		
	Lot of confidence	15	*
	Some confidence	48	*
	No real confidence	25	*
	Not sure	2	*

---

*Question was not asked.
†Includes high school students.

12

POLITICS AND POLITICAL VIEWS

Most noncollege youth are not finding it as easy to accept the political views of campus youth as they do the new social values. While it is evident that the less-educated sector of American youth has become increasingly critical of many aspects of American society, including major institutions, they still tend to be more conservative in their views about political issues and candidates than their college peers. Noncollege youth are, in fact, considerably less political than campus youth. Their politics are, if anything, pragmatic rather than idealistic, stemming in part from their own feelings that society is overly concerned with the needs of others (college students, minorities, etc.) and not enough with the needs of average young people who have to work for a living.

POLITICAL IDENTIFICATION AND OUTLOOK

Two qualities help to describe the different political outlooks and orientations of noncollege and college youth. While noncollege and college youth identify primarily with the Democratic rather than the Republican Party, noncollege youth are less likely to vote and are more conservative in their outlook than their college peers. In 1972, 48 percent of noncollege youth turned out on Election Day, in comparison with 74 percent of college youth. And a third of the noncollege youth, compared with only 21 percent of college youth, describe themselves as conservatives. (See Tables 29–1-2 and 30–1)

FUTURE VIETNAMS

On the prospects for future peace in the aftermath of the war in Vietnam, the views of noncollege and college youth are quite parellel. The one noteworthy difference is that a greater percentage of noncollege youth (17 percent) feel that the United States either won the Vietnam war or ended it with honor. Only 10 percent of the college youth expressed this same viewpoint. More striking than this one difference, however, is the marked similarity of the views of the two groups about the prospects for future peace. Eight out of ten young people, regardless of their educational background, have very little hope that we can look forward to a period of peace. Instead, they believe that involvements similar to Vietnam are inevitable. (Table 29–4)

VIEWS OF AMERICAN SOCIETY

While college and noncollege youth differ in their evaluation of certain institutions and in their stands on specific issues, in general the two groups start off with much the same overall estimate of American society:

A majority of both groups believe that the country is democratic in name only and run by special interests (58 percent noncollege, 63 percent college).

Only a minority in either instance believe that this is a sick society (35 percent both college and noncollege) or that it requires radical change (21 percent college, 25 percent noncollege).

Where they differ is in their evaluations of where the power in the country is vested. College youth see the giant corporations as the main power base in the country; noncollege youth believe that the power is more evenly balanced between Congress and big business. (Tables 29—5a-c and 30—2b)

Views of Specific Institutions

On campus, views of some American institutions have mellowed, primarily the military and the university. On the other hand, student skepticism continues at high levels.

Off campus, too, young people have become increasingly more skeptical about the viability of specific institutions—but their criticism, on the whole, still has not reached the same levels of acrimony expressed by college youth.

For example, while noncollege young people are just as critical of political parties as their college contemporaries, they are less critical of most other institutions including big business, the military, and the penal system. Interestingly, while they have found their high school experience to be less satisfactory than the college students, they are nowhere near as critical of the high school as an institution. One out of two college students (52 percent) believes that the high school system of education needs fundamental reform; only 38 percent of noncollege youth feel the same way.

One trend that should be noted, however, is the extent to which the views of the youth population have hardened:

In 1969, only 24 percent of noncollege youth found big business unviable as an institution. Today the figure is 45 percent. (In 1969, only 37 percent of college students found business unviable. Now the figure is 54 percent.)

Similarly, political parties were found to require fundamental reform by 44 percent of noncollege youth. Now the figure is 64 percent, a close match to the 61 percent figure for college youth. (Tables 29—5d and 30—2a)

Criticisms of the Critics

Noncollege youth are extremely critical of many aspects of American society, but on the other hand, they are equally angry at many of the people who are making these same criticisms.

On the one hand, noncollege youth agree as strongly as college students with the criticism that:

Business is too concerned with profits (noncollege 92 percent, college 94 percent).

People's privacy is being destroyed (noncollege 84 percent, college 86 percent).

Basically we are a racist nation (noncollege 77 percent, college 79 percent).

On the other hand, 78 percent of noncollege youth claim that they are "sick and tired of hearing people attack patriotism, morality, and traditional American values."

For many young people, the problem appears to be balancing their commitment to a solid, somewhat conservative viewpoint with their feelings that many aspects of American society need serious overhauling. Many of their attitudes reflect this conflict:

Noncollege youth have many criticisms of American political life and institutions—especially business—but they express faith in the American way of life.

They distrust American foreign policy—but not to the same extent as college youth. Still, an equal proportion of both groups (88 percent) agree that "our foreign policy is based on our own narrow economic and power interests."

More noncollege than college youth believe we are losing our right to dissent. Yet, they feel less alienated from society. They also say that the police should not hesitate to use force to maintain order (69 percent of noncollege youth subscribe to this notion versus 45 percent of college students) and that there is too much concern with equality and not enough with law and order (noncollege 71 percent, college 53 percent). (Table 29–5e)

Discrimination

Outside of the minority groups, most noncollege youth are somewhat less sensitive to the issue of discrimination than the college youth. For example, while 71 percent of the college youth feel that blacks are discriminated against, only 55 percent of all noncollege youth share this same feeling. An even more striking example is in the case of women. Almost six out of ten (58 percent) college students see women being discriminated against as a group. Among noncollege youth, only a minority (37 percent) feel this way. (Table 29–5f)

Support of Controversial Proposals

The more conservative and traditional political views of noncollege youth really come into focus in their attitudes toward such controversial issues as the death penalty, amnesty, and crackdown on pornography. In every instance, they take a more hard-line view than campus young people:

They are more in favor of the death penalty for certain crimes (noncollege 52 percent, college 44 percent).

They are more in favor of life sentences without parole for drug pushers (noncollege 45 percent, college 30 percent).

They are less in favor of legalizing marijuana (noncollege 47 percent, college 60 percent).

They are less in favor of amnesty for draft evaders (noncollege 42 percent, college 52 percent). (See Table 29−7)

PSYCHOLOGY OF ENTITLEMENT

Of potential political significance to the country is the fact that many benefits formerly treated as "wants" in life have become increasingly transformed among young people into a set of presumed "social rights." Interestingly, those off campus are about on a par with college students in calling for a "Bill of New Rights" including:

Best medical care, whether one can afford it or not (51 percent noncollege, 59 percent college).

Participation in job decisions (52 percent noncollege, 56 percent college).

Right to college for one's children (46 percent noncollege, 52 percent college).

Secure retirement (37 percent of both groups).

Right to a job (23 percent noncollege, 27 percent college).

Minimum income (22 percent noncollege, 26 percent college).

It is also interesting to note that this sense of entitlement is consistently greater among those in executive and professional positions than among white- or blue-collar workers, or even among college students as a whole. (Table 29−6)

ALIENATION

While noncollege youth have adopted the social and personal value system of the college campus, they continue to be considerably less alienated from American society than their better-educated peers. A majority (57 percent) of noncollege youth believe that their values are shared by most Americans, while only 40 percent of the college youth express this same feeling. Fewer of the noncollege youth (28 percent) would prefer to live in another country, in comparison with the 41 percent of the college students sharing this view. Interestingly, the foreign country of their choice is remarkably similar for college and noncollege youth who would sooner live in another country than the United States. In both instances, Canada is the number one choice, and countries with a different social system (i.e., China, Cuba, USSR) are barely even mentioned. Both South and North Vietnam are held in low esteem by both groups. (See Table 29–10)

IDENTIFICATION

Like their college peers, other young people between the ages of sixteen and twenty-five identify primarily with their families (61 percent noncollege, 68 percent college) and members of their own generation (68 percent noncollege, 61 percent college). However, only one out of two of the noncollege youth (46 percent) identifies strongly with students as a group. (See Tables 29–11 and 30–3-4)

TABLE 29   POLITICS AND POLITICAL VIEWS
By Total Noncollege Youth versus Total College Youth

	Total Noncollege %	Total College %
1. **Political Identification**		
a. *1972 Election†*		
Registered to vote	62	86
Voted	48	74
Nixon	23	31
McGovern	23	40
Other	1	2
Not sure	1	1

†Based on respondents 18 and over.

POLITICS AND POLITICAL VIEWS (Continued)

	Total Noncollege %	Total College %
b. *Party Identification*		
Democratic	45	49
Republican	21	24
Other	7	5
None	27	22
c. *Active in 1972 Campaign (Surveys, Rallies, Petitions, etc.)*	14	35
2. Political Outlook		
Conservative	13	7
Moderate/conservative	17	14
Moderate/middle-of-the-road	26	21
Liberal/middle-of-the-road	21	31
Liberal	19	22
Radical	4	5
3. View of Country		
Things are going very/fairly well	48	48
Things are going very/fairly badly	50	51
Not sure	2	1
4. View of Vietnam War		
a. *Feelings About End of War*		
We won the war	2	1
We ended the war with honor	15	9
We waited too long/could have gotten same results earlier	43	45
We lost the war—the communists will still take over South Vietnam	8	11
We suffered a moral loss—we had no right to be there	32	34
b. *View of Future*		
We can look forward to a period of peace	13	11
Similar military involvement is unavoidable	81	80
Not sure	6	9
5. Views of American Society		
a. *Nature of Our Society*		
We are a sick society	35	35

POLITICS AND POLITICAL VIEWS (Continued)

	Total Noncollege %	Total College %
Society is democratic in name only— special interests run things	58	63
b. *Own View of Society*		
American way of life is superior to life in other countries	19	12
There are flaws in our society, but we are flexible enough to solve them	56	67
System is not flexible; radical change is needed	18	17
Whole social system should be replaced	7	4
c. *Where Real Power Vested*		
Giant corporations	33	54
Congress	30	24
President	24	34
Financiers	16	30
General public	12	11
Special interest groups (i.e., labor, religious)	9	21
Defense Department	5	14
CIA	3	5
Republican Party	3	4
Democratic Party	2	2
d. *Institutions That Need Fundamental Reform or Elimination*		
Political parties	64	61
Penal system	50	69
Big business	45	54
Military	38	54
High schools	38	52
Trade unions	34	38
Congress	31	34
Mass media	27	27
FBI	27	37
Supreme Court	24	21
Universities and colleges	21	31
Constitution	13	12
e. *Criticism of American Society (Agree Strongly or Partially)*		
Business is too concerned with profits and not with public responsibility	92	94
Our foreign policy is based on our own narrow economic and power interests	88	88

POLITICS AND POLITICAL VIEWS (Continued)

	Total Noncollege %	Total College %
People's privacy is being destroyed	84	86
I am tired of hearing people attack patriotism, morality, American values	78	65
There is too much concern with the welfare "bum"	77	64
Basically we are a racist nation	77	79
We are rapidly losing our right to dissent	73	67
There is too much concern with equality and not enough with law and order	71	53
Police should not hesitate to use force to maintain order	69	55
The country pays too much attention to college students and not enough to other people	62	45
The Establishment unfairly controls every aspect of our lives	60	50
f. *Attention Paid to Minority Groups*		
Too much attention	27	28
Too little attention	38	41
Just right amount	27	24
Not sure	8	7
g. *Groups Discriminated Against by Society*		
American Indians	71	82
Homosexuals	66	82
Long-hairs	66	68
Poor people	64	71
Mexican-Americans	60	73
High school dropouts	60	59
Old people	57	62
Blacks	55	71
Women	37	58
Blue-collar workers	27	31
Vietnam veterans	24	24
People with foreign-born parents	23	23
College students	17	26

6. **Psychology of Entitlement**
   Entitled as a Social Right

	Total Noncollege %	Total College %
Best medical care (whether can afford it or not)	51	59
Participation in decisions that affect one's own work	52	56

POLITICS AND POLITICAL VIEWS (Continued)

	Total Noncollege %	Total College %
Sending children to college whether one can afford it or not	46	52
Secure retirement	37	37
Right to work	23	27
Minimum income	22	26
Interesting job	18	17

7. **Controversial Proposals Favored**

	Total Noncollege %	Total College %
Cutting back defense spending and using money for domestic needs	75	81
Stricter gun control	63	67
Death penalty for certain crimes	52	44
Legalizing marijuana	47	60
Life sentences without parole for drug pushers	45	30
Cracking down on pornography in movies, books, etc.	44	26
Amnesty for draft evaders	42	52
Limiting number of children a family can have	28	27
Using American money and know-how to help rebuild North Vietnam	23	25

8. **Countries Have Favorable Impression of:**

	Total Noncollege %	Total College %
Canada	79	86
England	68	78
Sweden	62	73
France	57	59
Mexico	54	56
Spain	50	48
Japan	48	*
West Germany	41	60
Greece	38	40
Argentina	34	36
Israel	32	44
Thailand	28	31
Chile	28	28
India	27	33

*Japan was not included in the college study.

POLITICS AND POLITICAL VIEWS (Continued)

	Total Noncollege %	Total College %
Formosa (Taiwan)	27	32
Egypt	22	16
Libya	21	20
Indonesia	21	23
Pakistan	18	17
Mainland China	17	26
Russia (USSR)	17	27
South Vietnam	16	14
East Germany	14	13
Cuba	10	12
North Vietnam	9	9

9. **Countries Have Unfavorable Impression of:**

North Vietnam	64	69
Russia (USSR)	54	46
Cuba	52	58
South Vietnam	44	52
East Germany	42	52
Mainland China	38	42
Egypt	31	52
Pakistan	28	41
Israel	28	33
India	19	26
Indonesia	19	23
Thailand	18	20
West Germany	17	12
Formosa (Taiwan)	16	21
Libya	15	25
Chile	14	23
Greece	12	24
Argentina	12	15
Japan	12	*
France	9	17
Mexico	8	9
Spain	8	18
Sweden	5	6
England	4	5
Canada	2	1

---

*Japan was not included in the college study.

POLITICS AND POLITICAL VIEWS (Continued)

		Total Noncollege %	Total College %
10.	**Alienation**		
	a. *Share Views with Most Americans*		
	Shared	57	40
	Not shared	28	43
	Not sure	15	17
	b. *Might Prefer to Live in Another Country*	28	41
	Canada	7	9
	Western Europe	4	4
	Australia	3	6
	Scandinavia	4	4
	Great Britain	2	5
	Cuba	**	**
	Other‡	8	13
	c. *Find a Conventional Life Intolerable*	12	13
11.	**Identification with:**		
	Other people of my generation	61	68
	Family	61	68
	Middle class	48	54
	Students	46	84
	Working class	44	27
	People in neighborhood	32	26
	People of my race	24	27
	People of my religion	23	28
	People of my nationality	22	30
	Liberals	20	36
	Conservatives	12	20
	Women's Liberation	9	15
	The Movement	7	6
	Counter Culture	6	8
	New Left	5	9
	Old Left	2	5

**Less than 0.5%.
‡Countries named by 1% of respondents.

TABLE 30 POLITICS AND POLITICAL VIEWS
Trend Data

	Noncollege		College	
	1973 %	1969 %	1973 %	1969 %
1. Party Identification				
Democratic	45	47	49	45
Republican	21	24	24	27
Other	7	5	5	5
Not sure	27	24	22	23
2. View of American Society				
a. Institutions That Need Fundamental Reform or Elimination				
Political parties	64	44	61	57
Big business	45	24	54	37
Military	38	31	54	61
Trade union	34	28	38	43
Mass media	27	26	27	35
Universities and colleges	21	28	31	32
b. Criticism of American Society (Agree Strongly or Partially)				
Business is too concerned with profits and not with public responsibility	92	92	94	93
Our foreign policy is based on our own narrow economic and power interests	88	73	88	83
There is too much concern with welfare "bum"	77	87	64	69
Basically we are a racist nation	77	73	79	77
There is too much concern with equality and not enough with law and order	71	82	53	57
The Establishment unfairly controls every aspect of our lives	60	56	50	58
3. Shared Views with Most Americans				
Shared	57	53	40	33
Not shared	28	28	43	31
Not sure	15	19	17	36

POLITICS AND POLITICAL VIEWS (Continued)

	Noncollege		College	
	1973 %	1969 %	1973 %	1969 %
4. Identification with:				
Other people of my generation	61	68	68	83
Family	61	75	68	78
Middle class	48	57	54	71
Students	46	48	84	88
People of my race	24	49	27	58
People of my religion	23	41	28	45
People of my nationality	22	38	30	54
Conservatives	12	14	20	23
New Left	5	3	9	13
Old Left	2	2	5	7

THREE
SOCIAL
PROFILES

13
MINORITIES

For this survey of young American adults, approximately 15 percent of those interviewed were nonwhite youth, mainly black.[1] The great majority of nonwhite youth do not go to college, a much larger proportion than among whites; therefore, the survey findings referred to here, unless otherwise noted, are limited to noncollege youth.

The picture of minority youth that emerges is one that differs in a number of respects from that of the majority of their white peers. Some of the differences tell a by-now familiar and unhappy story of low incomes, low education, and low expectations. Minority youth, like their parents, exhibit a stark statistical profile of less schooling, more unemployment, and a bleaker financial situation than their white peers. Their social views and personal values reflect these economic and educational differences. Minority youth tend to be more pessimistic than white youth about their immediate situations or future prospects. They look at society more critically, as a more hostile, more flawed environment; they would like to change society as a whole and many of its institutions and values in particular. They wear the labels "liberal" and "radical" more readily.

This is the familiar picture. A less familiar one also is projected by the survey findings—that of a group clinging strongly to some conservative beliefs

---

[1] Black youth make up three-quarters of the minority sampling, nearly one-fifth are Spanish speaking, and most of the rest are of Oriental origin.

and values. Markedly more than white youth, nonwhite young people attach importance to money, education, work, living a clean, moral life, and to traditional male and female roles and qualities.

Also, as the findings on college youth indicate, those minority youth who do go to college are at least as distinctive in their values and attitudes as are their white counterparts.

Here are some of the detailed differences between nonwhite youth and white youth and between nonwhite college students and nonwhite youth who do not go to college.

BACKGROUND

Minority youth come from less-advantaged homes than their white peers, not only in economic status, but also in their parents' educational backgrounds. Among minority youth, for example, almost two out of three (61 percent) have fathers who did not complete high school. This is twice the proportion for fathers of white noncollege youth. Similarly, 52 percent of the mothers of minority youth never completed high school, compared to only 29 percent of the general noncollege population. Minority youth themselves also acquire substanitally less formal education than whites. They drop out of high school twice as often as whites (26 percent to 12 percent). And minority youth, report a much higher rate of unemployment once they are out of school (16 percent compared to 10 percent). (See Table 31—1a-b)

PERSONAL OUTLOOK

Minority youth are substantially more troubled by their current financial situation and less optimistic than white youth about their future prospects. Only three out of five minority youth, compared to nearly four out of five whites, indicate things are going well in their personal lives. In other self-evaluations as well, these two groups give sharply different pictures of their current and future outlook in terms of whether they:

Are able to make ends meet (38 percent minority youth, 71 percent white youth).

See good opportunities in the future (57 percent minority youth, 79 percent white youth).

Are in control of their own future (48 percent minority youth, 66 percent white youth).

Have doubts about making as much money as they might want (55 percent minority, 40 percent white youth).

Have doubts about being as successful as they might want (39 percent minority youth, 26 percent white youth). (Table 31–2)

RACIAL AWARENESS

Part of the pessimism of nonwhite youth stems from their feeling that sizable obstacles confront them because of not being white in a largely white America. In fact, more than half (55 percent) feel their race would be a severe obstacle to getting a good job or advancing in their chosen career. The feeling that racial discrimination is still very much part of the American way of life is indicated in a number of other findings as well. This is a conviction that nonwhite youth harbor markedly more than white youth:

Three-quarters of minority youth feel that blacks are discriminated against; only one-half of white youth think so.

Forty-one percent of nonwhite youth strongly agree that we are a racist nation; only 23 percent of white youth do.

Sixty-nine percent of nonwhite youth feel that too little attention is paid to minority groups in the U.S.; less than half that number (32 percent) of whites say the same.

Greater sensitivity to discrimination by nonwhite youth extends to a feeling that many other groups are discriminated against as well. More than their white peers, minority youth think that women, blue-collar workers, old people, homosexuals, etc., are discriminated against. Also, but by relatively narrow margins, more nonwhites think that Mexican-Americans and American Indians are discriminated against.

As a corollary to discrimination, racial self-consciousness is also much higher among nonwhite youth than among white youth, as indicated by the wide gap between the percentage of each group that considers race a major grouping with which to identify (56 percent of nonwhite youth as compared with only 19 percent of white youth). (See Table 31–5b,d,e)

VIEW OF SOCIETY

By and large, minority youth are more cynical and critical of American society than are their white counterparts. This greater dissatisfaction is evidenced repeatedly throughout the survey in the different proportions of both groups that agree with propositions such as these:

This is a sick society (55 percent nonwhites, 31 percent whites).

The present system is largely democratic (24 percent nonwhites, 44 percent whites).

Things are going fairly well in the country (27 percent nonwhites, 48 percent whites).

Our society has flaws, but is flexible enough to solve them (30 percent nonwhites, 60 percent whites).

Man is good, but society corrupts (66 percent nonwhites, 48 percent whites).

Living in another country might be preferable (38 percent nonwhites, 26 percent whites).

Consistently enough, a larger proportion of nonwhite youth say they want to change society (42 percent compared to 25 percent among white youth), and in general more nonwhite youth are in favor of fundamental change for many basic American institutions, including political parties (50 percent nonwhites versus 45 percent of whites), the FBI (37 percent versus 20 percent), the Supreme Court (31 percent versus 19 percent) and the Constitution (19 percent versus 9 percent). Nonwhite youth indicate greater opposition to traditional sources of power and authority in general. Only 39 percent of minority youth say they accept the power and authority of police easily, for instance, compared to 64 percent of white youth. And 53 percent of minority youth say they accept the authority of a boss on the job easily, compared to 58 percent of whites. Related, too, is the notion that the "Establishment" unfairly controls our lives, an idea that a full three-quarters of minority youth subscribe to, compared to little over half of white youth. (See Table 31–3*d*,4,5*d*)

Political Outlook

The dissenting spirit of minority young people finds expression in their ideological self-classification. More than a third of this group, compared to only a fifth of white youth, see themselves as political liberals or radicals. Their stands on several important issues are consistently more liberal as well. More than half (57 percent) of nonwhite youth are opposed to the death penalty, while only about a third (37 percent) of whites take this position. Similarly, minority youth give substantially greater support to legalizing marijuana (55 percent compared to 46 percent for whites) and amnesty for draft evaders (54 percent compared to 40 percent among white youth). And, while neither group is predominantly in favor of a crackdown on pornography, minority youth give even less support (35 percent) than do whites (46 percent) to such a policy.

Minority young people take a more skeptical stance on the Vietnam War as well, with 41 percent believing we suffered a moral loss, compared to 30 percent among whites. But at the same time, nonwhite views run against the liberal grain in finding more reasons for going to war. Sizable portions of minority youth feel it is worth fighting in order to maintain a position of power (49 percent nonwhites versus 39 percent whites), our honor (55 percent versus 41 percent), and our national interests (60 percent versus 48 percent). (Table 31−5a,e,f)

Sex and Marriage

The New Values quest for sexual freedom and questions about the institution of marriage have found a more receptive audience among minority youth than among whites. Nearly two out of three nonwhites—compared to only two out of five whites—say they welcome more acceptance of sexual freedom. Minority youth also have less confidence (51 percent versus 64 percent for white youth) that marriage is still a viable institution. Moreover, the practice of having children outside of formal marriage is condemned much less often by minority youth (44 percent) than by white youth (61 percent).

Interestingly, these differences in attitudes about marriage do not distinguish the two groups' expressed desire to have children (anticipated by three-quarters of each group). Once married, moreover, neither group sanctions infidelity to any great extent. In this regard, the moral norms of nonwhite youth are even more critical than whites of extramarital sex in general (condemned by 74 percent and 67 percent respectively). Yet, the reverse is true for mate-swapping, which is criticized by 73 percent of whites and 64 percent of nonwhites. (Table 31−3a-b)

Men and Women

Nonwhite youth may be generally more liberal in their attitudes and values surrounding sex and marriage, but they appear to be significantly more conservative about men and women with regard to their natures and roles. They are less receptive to most Women's Liberation ideas, for instance, including these propositions:

"Women's place is in the home" is nonsense (accepted by 59 percent white youth, 44 percent nonwhite youth).

A woman does not need a man to be happy (accepted by 50 percent whites, 48 percent nonwhites).

Women should be free to take the initiative in sex (accepted by 85 percent whites, 75 percent nonwhites).

Nonwhite attitudes toward men and masculine qualities diverge even further and more consistently from those of white youth. The following proportions of white and nonwhite youth feel that a man should:

Be physically strong (24 percent whites versus 49 percent nonwhites).

Make decisions about family matters (38 percent versus 54 percent).

Keep his feeling under control (46 percent versus 62 percent).

Show women courtesy and respect (60 percent versus 77 percent).

(See Table 31–3*b-c*)

More Traditional Norms Remain

In addition to adhering to more traditional attitudes about men and women, minority youth are significantly more traditional in the importance they attach to a number of other conventional values. There is, for example, a sharp difference in the importance attached to money, with minority youth specifying that money is a very important personal value more than twice as often as white youth (62 percent to only 29 percent). Other things to which minority youth attach substantially greater importance than whites include:

Education (87 percent minority youth versus 73 percent white youth).

Work (68 percent versus 50 percent).

A clean, moral life (68 percent versus 55 percent).

Religion (48 percent versus 41 percent).

Privacy (87 percent versus 76 percent).

Duty before pleasure (75 percent versus 64 percent).

Perhaps it is a matter of being resigned or discouraged, but while a significantly larger portion of nonwhite youth are for changing society and its established ways and institutions, there are also more nonwhites than whites who seem to see little personal benefit in challenging the status quo. To the notion that people who accept things as they exist are better off than those who do not, 29 percent of white youth agree, while a full 45 percent of nonwhite youth subscribe to this particularly conservative belief. (Table 31–3)

COLLEGE VERSUS NONCOLLEGE MINORITY YOUTH

All of the above findings on minority youth refer to noncollege youth, who make up the great majority of the minority youth population. But in addition, there is a small but important subgroup within minority youth ranks—those who go to college. Their numbers are growing on campus, and if the pattern of college students leading the way in changes in attitudes and values should hold for nonwhite youth as well as whites, the survey findings about minority youth in college may tell a good deal about the course of minority youth overall, especially those findings that indicate distinct difference between college and noncollege minority youth.

There are many such findings, and they suggest generally that nonwhite youth in college tend to be closer to the white majority of students than do nonwhite youth who do not go to college. This implies that social class influences may be stronger than group solidarity. In many areas, in fact, college youth, white and nonwhite, hold viewpoints closer to one another than either group does to its noncollege counterpart. This is understandable enough in matters concerning higher education itself, so it is not surprising to find that college whites and nonwhites are closer together in questioning the viability of colleges and universities—only 15 and 12 percent respectively feel that these institutions need no substantial change. Noncollege youth are proportionally closer in finding colleges and universities adequate the way they are (31 percent noncollege whites, 28 percent noncollege nonwhites).

These parallels extend to areas well beyond concerns that distinguish college from noncollege youth to begin with. College whites and nonwhites are close to each other and a sizable gap away from their noncollege counterparts in thinking, for instance:

That the military needs fundamental change or should be done away with entirely. More than half of both groups in college think so, compared to less than 40 percent of both groups not in college.

That the penal system should be fundamentally reformed or done away with. Close to seven out of ten of both whites and nonwhites in college think so, compared to about five out of ten of both whites and nonwhites who do not go to college.

That our national honor is worth fighting for. Like white students, relatively few nonwhite students subscribe to this idea (19 percent and 22 percent respectively), while both whites and nonwhites who do not go to college express much more support (41 percent and 55 percent).

Greater Difference Than Whites

Nonwhite college students in general, like white students, tend to be more liberal, to be more critical of society and of traditional ways than their noncollege peers. Noncollege minority youth, as noted earlier, tend to be more liberal and more critical, in turn, than noncollege white youth. So, broadly speaking, there is often a progression of attitudes from noncollege whites to college nonwhites. Where 31 percent of whites who are not in college think this is a sick society, for instance, 55 percent of minority youth who are not in college subscribe to this indictment, and 60 percent of minority youth who are in college feel the same way. By comparison, only 32 percent of white students think this is a sick society, hardly more than noncollege youth.

Minority college students are often further apart from their noncollege peers than white students are. Take two examples:

"Cheating big companies is morally wrong." This proposition is supported by 72 percent of noncollege minority youth, but by only half that proportion of minority youth in college (35 percent). The difference between noncollege and college white youth is much smaller (61 percent versus 52 percent).

While more than half of noncollege minority youth find it easy to accept the power and authority of a boss on the job, less than a quarter of college nonwhites do. The range again is much smaller between white youth who do not go to college and those who do (58 percent versus 46 percent).

More Like Each Other

There is one major area in which minority youth in and out of college tend to be more like each other than their college or noncollege white counterparts. This is the broad realm of attitudes about sex and about male and female qualities. As noted earlier, minority youth place more stress on traditional masculine characteristics and tend to be less liberated in their viewpoints about women. This is true of both college and noncollege minority youth. Sometimes, unlike white youth, minority youth in college are either just as traditional in their viewpoints about such matters as their noncollege counterparts or even more so:

> Both in and out of college, 47 percent of nonwhite youth feel it is an important quality in a man that he "can't be pushed around by women," while markedly fewer college whites feel this way than do noncollege white youth (30 percent versus 39 percent).

> The opinion that a woman's place is in the home is regarded as nonsense by more noncollege minority youth than by their college counterparts (46 percent versus 44 percent), while more college than noncollege whites think so (59 percent versus 54 percent).

> Fewer college than noncollege minority youth would welcome more acceptance of sexual freedom (57 percent versus 63 percent), while more white college youth would than noncollege youth (66 percent versus 44 percent).

Overall, comparisons of college and noncollege survey results indicate that nonwhite youth are hardly monolithic, that a good deal of difference in attitudes and values exists among minority young people, depending on which side of the college gates they are found.

TABLE 31   MINORITIES—SUMMARY TABLE
By White versus Nonwhite Noncollege Youth

	Total White %	Total Nonwhite %
1. Background Differences		
a. Parents' Backgrounds		
Mothers did not complete high school	29	52
Fathers did not complete high school	34	61
Fathers are blue-collar	48	69

MINORITIES—SUMMARY TABLE (Continued)

		Total White %	Total Nonwhite %
b.	*Own Status*		
	Some college education	27	18
	High school dropout	12	26
	Kind of education†		
	General	36	49
	College preparatory	22	14
	Vocational, technical	14	17
	Employment		
	Employed 20 hours or more	44	43
	Employed part time	2	5
	Housewife (not employed)	14	10
	High school student	<u>30</u>	<u>27</u>
	Employed	18	20
	Not employed	12	7
	Unemployed	10	16
	Vietnam veteran	6	12
2.	**Personal Outlook**		
	Things going well in personal life	78	60
	Able to make ends meet	71	38
	Had the right amount of education	33	13
	Have good opportunities in future	79	57
	Have doubts about making as much money as wanted in the future	40	55
	Have doubts about being as successful as wanted	26	39
	Race a barrier to job	7	55
3.	**Value Differences**		
a.	*Very Important Personal Values*		
	Education	73	87
	Doing things for others	65	58
	Living a clean, moral life	55	68
	Work	50	68
	Patriotism	41	34
	Religion	41	48
	Money	29	62
	Changing society	25	42

† Asked of respondents who completed grade school but did not go to college.

MINORITIES—SUMMARY TABLE (Continued)

	Total White %	Total Nonwhite %
b. *Male-Female Relations*		
Would welcome more acceptance of sexual freedom	44	63
Believe marriage is not obsolete	64	51
Look forward to being married	49	46
Look forward to having children	79	76
c. *Activities Thought to Be Morally Wrong*		
Interchanging partners among couples	73	64
Using violence to achieve worthwhile ends	74	65
Extramarital sexual relations	67	74
Having children without formal marriage	61	44
Cheating big companies	66	61
d. *Belief in Traditional American Values*		
Duty comes before pleasure	64	75
Man is good, society corrupts	48	65
People who accept things are better off than those who do not	29	45
4. Alienation		
Have values not shared by most Americans	28	30
Would prefer to live in another country	26	38
5. Political Views and Attitudes		
a. *Political Outlook*		
Conservative	13	13
Moderate conservative	17	12
Moderate/middle-of-the-road	27	20
Liberal/middle-of-the-road	21	20
Liberal	18 }21	27 }34
Radical	3	7
b. *View of Society*		
Believe this is sick society	31	55
Present system largely democratic	44	24
Too little attention paid to minorities	32	69
c. *Vietnam*		
We suffered a moral loss	30	41
d. *Criticism of American Society (Agree Strongly or Partially)*		
Basically we are a racist nation	76	83

MINORITIES—SUMMARY TABLE (Continued)

	Total White %	Total Nonwhite %
The Establishment unfairly controls our lives	51	75
We are rapidly losing our right to dissent	72	80
e. Groups Discriminated Against by Society		
Poor people	61	81
High school dropouts	57	73
Blacks	51	74
Women	36	46
Blue-collar workers	25	35
Vietnam veterans	22	38
f. Controversial Issues Favored		
Death penalties for certain crimes	55	36
Legalizing marijuana	46	55
Amnesty for draft evaders	40	54
Cracking down on pornography	46	35

14
VETERANS

Approximately 7 percent of the noncollege youth sample (15 percent of males in the sample) report having served in Vietnam. And these veterans, we find, sharply differ in attitudes and values from other noncollege people their age; they also differ markedly in their social and economic backgrounds.

The veterans in our sample report nearly double the unemployment rate of other noncollege youth, and they consistently describe their personal situation in more negative terms. They are more discouraged over what the future holds for them. And they reflect a relatively greater estrangement from American society than do their peers.

MORAL AND SOCIAL VIEWS

These veterans are considerably less strict in their moral viewpoints than other young people outside of college. On numerous social and political questions, too, they take a relatively less traditional, more liberal stance. However, the veterans are more conservative on war-related issues. They are more strongly opposed than are their peers to amnesty for draft evaders, and they overwhelmingly disapprove of using American aid to help rebuild North Vietnam.

Here are details from the sample of America's Vietnam veterans.

Demographic Differences

The Vietnam veterans differ from other noncollege youth in several important respects:

Veterans report a sharply higher rate of unemployment (33 percent veterans compared to 17 percent others).

There are more minority youth among the veterans (26 percent veterans compared to 16 percent overall).

More of the veterans' fathers have less than a high school education (57 percent veterans compared to 43 percent overall).

Veterans less often come from high schools where most students go to college (32 percent veterans compared to 47 percent overall). (See Table 32–1)

Personal Outlook

In terms of their personal problems and financial situation, Vietnam veterans are considerably less well off and less optimistic about the future than are their peers as these responses indicate:

Things are going well in personal life (52 percent veterans compared to 74 percent others).

Able to make ends meet financially (46 percent veterans compared to 63 percent others).

Have good opportunities for the future (63 percent veterans compared to 73 percent others). (Table 32–2)

Alcohol and Drugs

As a measure of their discontent, perhaps, veterans report far heavier use of alcohol and drugs. Nearly half (45 percent) of the veterans interviewed reported that they had drunk a lot over the previous weekend; only one-fifth of other noncollege youth said they had. And twice as many veterans said they had gotten high on drugs (17 percent versus 8 percent). (Table 32–3)

Self-Evaluation

The veterans' relative pessimism about their present situation and future outlook is confirmed by their responses to other self-evaluation questions:

On the whole, I'm satisfied with myself (65 percent veterans, 72 percent others).

I feel trapped by my lack of training (27 percent veterans, 20 percent others).

I'm pretty discouraged about the future (24 percent veterans, 18 percent others).

I feel like a second-class citizen (25 percent veterans, 14 percent others).

The veterans group also shows less satisfaction with the education they have received.

Had the right amount of education (16 percent veterans, 26 percent others).

Had the right kind of education (52 percent veterans, 69 percent others). (Table 32–4)

Barriers Toward Getting Work

Consistent with their dissatisfaction about the education they have had, Vietnam veterans also are more sensitive to lack of education as an obstacle to getting a good job. Educational background is cited as a job barrier by 52 percent of the veterans and 46 percent of other youth. Lack of vocational training in particular is mentioned by 47 percent of the veterans, compared to 39 percent of the others.

The veterans also seem more sensitive to possible problems in employment resulting from their attitudes toward authority (33 percent veterans, 22 percent others), unwillingness to conform (25 percent veterans, 19 percent others), and their political views (18 percent veterans, just 6 percent others). (Table 32–5)

Moral Issues

The veterans are consistently less strict in their moral structures than are others their age who do not go to college. On sex-related questions, for example, they are less likely to morally condemn actions such as:

Extramarital sex (condemned by only 45 percent of veterans, 63 percent others).

Having children without formal marriage (50 percent veterans, 56 percent others).

Having an abortion (39 percent veterans, 47 percent others).

Homosexual relations (35 percent veterans, 43 percent others).

Premarital sex (12 percent veterans, 30 percent others).

On other ethical questions, the Vietnam veterans also are not as strict as other noncollege youth:

Collecting welfare when you could work (criticized by 75 percent veterans, 82 percent others).

Selling dope to pay for college (69 percent veterans, 80 percent others).

Using violence to achieve worthwhile results (60 percent veterans, 72 percent others).

Cheating big companies (56 percent veterans, 65 percent others).
(See Table 32–6)

Alienation

The Vietnam veterans more often feel that their values are not shared by most other Americans (35 percent to 30 percent for others). The veterans are also more willing to give up living in this country for some other country or society (37 percent compared to 29 percent). (Table 32–7)

Ideological Self-Classification

The Vietnam veterans are found more often than their peers at the extremes of the political spectrum, especially the radical end. They see themselves as conservatives 19 percent of the time, compared to 12 percent for others. And 15 percent of the veterans identify themselves as political radicals, in contrast to just 4 percent over all. (Table 32–8a)

Controversial Issues

On some issues, the veterans take a more liberal position than their peers, while on others they are decidedly more conservative. On the liberal side:

Life sentences without parole for drug pushers (supported by just 34 percent of veterans, compared to 45 percent of others).

Cutting defense spending and using money for domestic needs (83 percent veterans, 76 percent others).

Legalizing marijuana (76 percent veterans, 49 percent others).

On the conservative side, undoubtedly related to their military experience:

Amnesty for draft evaders (supported by just 33 percent of veterans, 43 percent of others).

Using American money and know-how to help rebuild North Vietnam (10 percent veterans, 21 percent others).

Stricter gun control (46 percent veterans, 62 percent others).

(See Table 32–8*b*)

Groups Discriminated Against

The veterans are more attuned to problems of social discrimination:

Long hairs (discrimination perceived by 76 percent of veterans, only 35 percent of others).

Blacks (62 percent veterans, 54 percent others).

Blue-collar workers (36 percent veterans, 28 percent others).

However, the sharpest difference occurs in 37 percent of veterans perceiving themselves as discriminated against, whereas any 24 percent of others feel that this is so. (Table 32–8*c*)

Social Restraints

When it comes to the various restraints and controls imposed by society, the veterans group is comparatively more resentful than their peers.

Prohibitions against marijuana (easily accepted by 49 percent overall, but only 38 percent of veterans).

Conforming in matters of dress and personal grooming (42 percent overall, 32 percent of veterans).

Outward conformity for the sake of career or job advancement (35 percent overall, 26 percent of veterans).

(Table 32–8*d*)

War and Peace

As a striking comment on the frustration of the Vietnam conflict felt by those closest to it, veterans are half as likely as their peers (7 percent to 13 percent) to feel the war was ended with honor, and say more than twice as often that we lost it altogether (23 percent to 9 percent). As for the chances for future peace, the veterans are even more pessimistic than other young people. Fully nine out of ten, compared to eight out of ten overall, feel that similar military involvements like Vietnam are inevitable. For that matter, the veterans of America's latest war are more in favor of going to war again:

To counteract aggression (68 percent veterans, 55 percent others).

To contain communism (54 percent veterans, 48 percent others).

To protect allies (59 percent veterans, 45 percent others).

(Table 32—8*f*)

TABLE 32   VETERANS
By Total Noncollege Youth Not in High School
versus Vietnam Veterans

	Total Noncollege Youth Not in High School %	Total Vietnam Veterans %
1. Background Differences		
Father did not complete high school	43	57
White	84	74
Nonwhite	16	26
Came from high school where most students go to college	47	32
Unemployed (excluding housewives)	17	33
2. Personal Outlook		
Things going well in personal life	74	52
Able to make ends meet financially	62	46
Had the right amount of education	26	16
Had the right kind of education	69	52
Have good opportunities in the future	73	63
Have clear plans for the future	64	45

VETERANS (Continued)

	Total Noncollege Youth Not in High School %	Total Vietnam Veterans %
3. Drugs		
Drank a lot over past weekend	20	45
Got high on drugs over past weekend	8	17
4. Self-Evaluation		
On the whole I'm satisfied with myself	72	65
I'm in control of my own future	63	56
I feel trapped by my lack of training	20	27
I feel pretty discouraged about the future	18	24
I just can't get ahead	16	28
I'm wasting my time and not getting anywhere	17	25
I feel like a second-class citizen	14	25
5. Barriers to a Desirable Job		
Educational background	46	52
Lack of vocational training	39	47
Attitudes toward authority	22	33
Unwillingness to conform	19	25
Sex	16	1
Race	14	21
Political views	6	18
Family background	6	5
Religion	3	—
None of these	24	14
6. Value Differences		
a. Activities Thought to Be Morally Wrong		
Collecting welfare when you could work	82	75
Selling dope to pay for college	80	69
Using violence to achieve worthwhile results	72	60
Cheating big companies	65	56
Extramarital sexual relations	63	45
Having children without formal marriage	56	50
Having an abortion	47	39
Relations between consenting homosexuals	43	35
Casual premarital sexual relations	30	12

VETERANS (Continued)

		Total Noncollege Youth Not in High School %	Total Vietnam Veterans %
b.	*Belief in Traditional American Values*		
	People should save money regularly	80	75
	Private property is sacred	75	70
	Competition encourages excellence	66	85
	Hard work always pays off	53	45
	Man is good, but society corrupts	50	57
7.	**Alienation**		
	Have values not shared by most other Americans	30	35
	Would prefer to live in another country	29	37
8.	**Political Views and Attitudes**		
a.	*Political Outlook*		
	Conservative	12	19
	Moderate/conservative	15	15
	Moderate/middle-of-the-road	26	17
	Liberal/middle-of-the-road	23	16
	Liberal	19	17
	Radical	4	15
b.	*Controversial Proposals Favored*		
	Life sentences without parole for drug pushers	45	34
	Cutting defense spending and using money for domestic needs	76	83
	Stricter gun control	62	46
	Legalizing marijuana	49	76
	Amnesty for draft evaders	43	33
	Using American money and know-how to help rebuild North Vietnam	21	10
c.	*Groups Discriminated Against by Society*		
	Long-hairs	65	76
	Blacks	54	62
	Blue-collar workers	28	36
	Vietnam veterans	24	37

VETERANS (Continued)

	Total Noncollege Youth Not in High School %	Total Vietnam Veterans %
d. *Restraints Willingly and Easily Accepted*		
Prohibition against marijuana	49	38
Conformity in matters of dress and personal grooming	42	32
Outward conformity for the sake of career or job advancement	35	26
e. *Vietnam*		
We won the war	2	1
We ended the war with honor	13	7
We waited too long	41	38
We lost the war	9	23
We suffered a moral loss	34	28
Not sure	1	3
Similar military involvements are unavoidable	82	91
f. *Reasons Worth Fighting a War for*		
Counteracting aggression	55	68
Containing communism	48	54
Protecting our allies	45	59

15
NONCOLLEGE GROUPINGS

In recent years, there has been a tendency to talk about American youth as though they formed a single group with a single outlook. But as earlier chapters have indicated, there are substantial differences between youth groupings, be they college women, noncollege youth in general, veterans, or minority college students. The survey on which this book is based found numerous, almost countless divisions and differences. Geographic ones for instance. Young noncollege Americans living in the Northeast and Far West tend to be more liberal, more critical about society. Four out of ten such youth in both regions think ours is a sick society, for instance, compared with three out of ten in the north central and southern parts of the country.

There are also marked differences in viewpoint that depend on how young the people surveyed are. Not surprisingly, within the sixteen- to twenty-five-year-old age span of the survey, the younger the respondent, the more optimistic and idealistic he or she tended to be. When asked if they thought women were discriminated against, only a third of sixteen- and seventeen-year-olds, for instance, said they thought so, whereas nearly half of those in the twenty-two- to twenty-five-year-old bracket feel that such discrimination exists.

It would take volumes to give all the possible comparisons between all the possible groupings covered by the survey, but several noncollege groupings, in addition to those already looked at, are of particular interest and importance, and this final chapter focuses on them: high school students, the employed, the unemployed, and housewives.

HIGH SCHOOL STUDENTS

High school students are more positive than other segments of noncollege youth about the state of the country and, generally, render a less critical diagnosis of our major social and political institutions. The majority see things going well in the nation (59 percent compared with only 43 percent of other noncollege youth), and they are also stronger believers in the democratic nature of the system. These views are backed by a relatively greater conviction that Congress and the public at large hold much of the power in the country, while giant corporations and financial institutions are seen as the real power-brokers by other noncollege young people. High school youth also see less need for reform in such major institutions as our political parties (58 percent to 65 percent for other noncollege youth), the penal system (43 percent to 53 percent), big business (37 percent to 48 percent), and the military (32 percent to 40 percent).

In their personal values and moral outlook, high school youth hold more traditional moral views than the somewhat older group. A greater number of them stress the desirability of living a "clean, moral life," and view such sex-related issues as extramarital relations, children outside formal marriage, and premarital sex as morally reprehensible. This moral outlook also extends to support for the idea that hard work always pays off (63 percent compared with 53 percent of other noncollege youth) and that duty should come before pleasure (70 percent to 64 percent). Rounding out this picture of high school youth is the finding that they more often feel their own values are shared by most other Americans (62 percent to 55 percent). (Table 33)

THE EMPLOYED AND THE UNEMPLOYED

There are sharp demographic differences setting unemployed young people apart from those with jobs. The unemployed include proportionately more minority youths than do the employed (21 percent compared to 15 percent), and unemployed youth come more often from lower socioeconomic backgrounds. Nearly half (47 percent) report their fathers never finished high school, compared to 38 percent for the employed, and more than a third are high school dropouts themselves.

Not surprisingly, unemployed youth report greater financial difficulties than other youth and do not feel as satisfied with their personal lives. While seven out of ten of those employed indicate little difficulty in making ends meet, less than half (45 percent) of the unemployed are so fortunate. Also, a full three-quarters of those with jobs, in contrast to 60 percent of the unemployed, say things are going well in their personal lives.

In their personal and social outlook, unemployed youth are somewhat less ardent defenders of traditional moral norms than are the employed. Although the differences are not great, it is the employed who are more concerned with issues of law and order, respect for authority, and the desire for less permissiveness. It is also the employed who more staunchly believe that doing any job well is important, that people should save regularly, and that competition leads to excellence. And finally, the employed are relatively more stringent in their moral views—more often condemning such actions as destroying private property, stealing, collecting welfare when one can work, cheating big companies, and marital transgression.

The unemployed also express less overall attachment to American society than do young people with jobs. They feel less comfortable accepting a conventional life style and less often feel their values are shared by other Americans. Indeed, a substantial portion of the unemployed (38 percent compared to 26 percent of the employed) indicate they would just as soon live in some other country or society.

In political outlook, this relative alienation of the unemployed is expressed in terms of a wider feeling that this is a sick society (39 percent to 33 percent of the employed) and that radical change is needed in the system (35 percent to 21 percent of the employed).

The two groups share many criticisms of society and politics, but there also are significant areas of difference. Those with jobs are much harsher in their views of current welfare policy, and also give more support to the use of force by police. The unemployed, on the other hand, are less satisfied with certain major social institutions, such as the mass media, the FBI, the Supreme Court, and the Constitution. The unemployed are also more sensitive to the issue of social discrimination—particularly against blacks and high school dropouts. Concerning two other controversies—legalization of marijuana and the death penalty—the unemployed take a more liberal stand than do those with jobs.

Finally, unemployed youths were much less likely to register and vote in the last presidential election. When they did make it to the polls, their votes were cast by nearly a 2 to 1 margin for McGovern, while the employed group split almost evenly between the two candidates. (Table 33)

HOUSEWIVES

Demographically, the young housewives come from backgrounds with a somewhat lower level of education than other noncollege subgroups. More than half (54 percent) say their fathers did not finish high school, and more than one out of three (35 percent) housewives dropped out before they themselves finished high school.

These young women are not faring as well financially as most of their peers, although this does not seem to carry over into dissatisfaction with their personal lives. Just slightly over half (55 percent compared to 66 percent overall) say they are able to make ends meet financially, while 77 percent report things are going well in their personal lives. The financial plight of the young housewife does make itself felt, however, in her future outlook, with just 68 percent (compared to 75 percent of her peers) seeing good opportunities for getting ahead in the future.

There are signs of frustration in the self-evaluation of young homemakers—centering chiefly on the feeling that they are somewhat inferior and that they are not getting the most out of life. However, these frustrations are not translated into a direct concern for self-fulfillment, as promoted by Women's Liberation advocates. Rather, as paramount among their future priorities, the young housewives are overwhelmingly concerned with economic security and providing for their families (74 percent compared to 57 percent for noncollege youth.)

There are numerous other indications of the young housewives' greater commitment to traditional norms. As important personal values, they more often mention such concerns as family (87 percent compared to 81 percent overall), living a clean and moral life (69 percent to 57 percent), having children (64 percent to just 45 percent), religion (55 percent to 42 percent), and patriotism (52 percent to 40 percent).

The young homemakers are also much more keen on the need for law and order (80 percent compared to 68 percent among noncollege youth) and respect for authority (80 percent to 66 percent overall). At the same time, they are much less accepting than their peers of value changes such as the trend toward sexual freedom, and they more often condemn such practices as mate-swapping (80 percent), extramarital sex (72 percent), having children without formal marriage (65 percent), abortion (62 percent), and, to a lesser extent, premarital sex (42 percent).

Consistent with their more traditional outlook, young housewives find it easier than most young people to accept a conventional life style, and they are less resistant to many of the restraints and controls imposed by society. They are, for example, more accepting of the power and authority of the police (69 percent to 60 percent for total noncollege youth), settling down to a routine (60 percent to 47 percent), and conforming in matters of personal dress and grooming (49 percent to 42 percent overall).

Young housewives are also relatively conservative on the subject of many of today's controversies, such as legalization of marijuana (endorsed by only 30 percent compared to 47 percent overall), amnesty for draft evaders (36 percent to 42 percent overall), and life sentences for drug pushers (59 percent to 45 percent overall). They are also somewhat less sympathetic to problems of minority groups.

In the last presidential election, young housewives turned out to register and vote less often than other noncollege youth. When they did vote, their support went overwhelmingly to Mr. Nixon.

TABLE 33   NONCOLLEGE GROUPINGS

	Non-college Total %	High School Students %	Employed %	Unemployed %	Housewives %
1. Background Differences					
a. Race					
White	85	87	85	79	88
Nonwhite	15	13	15	21	12
b. Father's Education					
Less than high school	39	29	38	47	54
High school or more	61	71	62	53	46
c. Mother's Education					
Less than high school	33	25	33	36	48
High school or more	67	75	67	64	52

NONCOLLEGE GROUPINGS (Continued)

		Non-college Total %	High School Students %	Employed %	Unemployed %	House-wives %
d.	*Father's Occupation*					
	Professional/executive/managerial	27	33	29	20	15
	White-collar	16	16	17	17	13
	Blue-collar	51	47	49	52	61
	Other/retired/unemployed	6	4	5	11	11
e.	*Respondent's Education*					
	Less than high school	*	*	12	32	35

2. Personal Outlook

		Non-college Total %	High School Students %	Employed %	Unemployed %	House-wives %
a.	*Presently able to make ends meet*	66	74	69	45	55
b.	*Things going well in own life*	75	79	76	61	77
c.	*See good opportunities to get ahead in future*	75	81	77	63	68
d.	*Have no doubts about being as successful as I want*	72	74	75	62	68
e.	*Had right kind of education*	69	69	72	58	66
f.	*Self-Evaluation*					
	I enjoy life very much	75	75	78	62	79
	I'm satisfied with myself	72	72	76	62	67
	I'm in control of my future	63	65	63	57	61
	I'm more concerned with myself than with the world	39	34	41	47	38
	I do things better than most people	36	38	40	29	25

*Based on respondents 18 and over.

NONCOLLEGE GROUPINGS (Continued)

	Non-college Total %	High School Students %	Em-ployed %	Unem-ployed %	House-wives %
I like to be independent but I can't	23	28	17	25	29
I feel uncomfortable with people with more education	19	19	17	18	27
I feel trapped by lack of training	18	13	19	23	22
I'm pretty discouraged about the future	18	18	14	28	20
I feel kind of left out of things	18	18	13	21	27
I just can't get ahead	16	16	11	25	24
I'm wasting time, not getting anywhere	16	13	16	26	14
I feel like a second-class citizen	15	16	12	18	15
I never got the guidance I needed	14	13	13	21	18
What I think doesn't count	13	17	8	18	15
I'm a political person	12	12	11	12	6
I rarely get a chance to enjoy myself	11	10	9	10	20
I find life pretty dull	10	10	8	14	14
g. *Future Priorities* Economic security and providing for my family comes first	57	56	55	45	74
I'm not that concerned with economic security. I guess I take it for granted. I'm more concerned with doing things that will give me a sense of self-fulfillment	43	54	45	55	26

NONCOLLEGE GROUPINGS (Continued)

	Non-college Total %	High School Students %	Em-ployed %	Unem-ployed %	House-wives %
3. Value Differences					
a. Very Important Personal Values					
Love	88	84	90	82	94
Fulfilling yourself as a person	87	85	88	87	87
Friendship	87	89	86	89	82
Family	81	76	84	75	87
Privacy	78	74	77	78	86
Education	75	78	73	66	79
Doing things for others	64	64	61	65	69
Being close to nature	50	47	49	55	52
Living a clean, moral life	57	62	51	53	69
Work	53	57	50	55	49
Being creative	52	46	54	59	54
Having children	45	39	43	47	64
Religion	42	45	37	37	55
Patriotism	40	43	37	34	52
Money	34	33	34	36	34
Changing society	27	27	27	32	27
b. Welcome Social Changes					
More emphasis on self-expression	76	75	78	77	69
Less emphasis on money	74	69	74	77	76
More emphasis on law and order	68	68	66	58	80
More respect for authority	66	67	64	53	80
More emphasis on traditional family ties	61	52	64	59	75
More acceptance of sexual freedom	47	44	51	53	30
Less emphasis on working hard	35	36	32	40	34

NONCOLLEGE GROUPINGS (Continued)

	Non-college Total %	High School Students %	Em-ployed %	Unem-ployed %	House-wives %
Less emphasis on permissiveness	33	31	36	26	33
More acceptance of drug usage	15	17	17	24	10
c. Belief in Traditional American Values					
Doing any job well is important	89	89	89	80	93
Business is entitled to make a profit	85	85	86	80	86
People should save money regularly	80	78	80	73	86
Commitment to a meaningful career is very important	79	80	79	77	76
Private property is sacred	74	74	74	76	76
A "strong" person can control own life	70	70	73	62	66
Competition encourages excellence	66	67	70	62	58
Duty comes before pleasure	66	70	63	61	75
Hard work always pays off	56	63	52	50	57
Man is basically good, but society corrupts	50	52	49	57	44
d. Activities Thought to Be Morally Wrong					
Destroying private property	88	88	90	81	89
Taking things without paying for them	88	88	89	80	90
Collecting welfare when you could work	83	84	84	73	83

NONCOLLEGE GROUPINGS (Continued)

	Non-college Total %	High School Stu-dents %	Em-ployed %	Unem-ployed %	House-wives %
Paying for college by selling dope	80	80	81	66	87
Interchanging partners among couples	72	75	69	65	80
Using violence to achieve worthwhile results	73	73	72	69	75
Cheating big compa-nies	66	66	67	57	69
Extramarital sexual relations	65	70	63	54	72
Having children with-out formal marriage	58	64	56	44	65
Living with a spouse you do not love	52	53	51	53	50
Having an abortion	48	51	43	42	62
Relations between con-senting homosexuals	47	56	41	39	48
Casual premarital sex-ual relations	34	43	27	24	42

4. **Alienation**
   a. *Believe Views Are Not Shared by Most Americans*

Americans	28	23	32	34	23

   b. *Conventional Life Style*

Same kind of life as my parents	12	15	9	9	13
No difficulty in accept-ing kind of life society has to offer	63	59	66	48	72
Not going to be easy to accept conven-tional life style	12	14	11	18	6

NONCOLLEGE GROUPINGS (Continued)

		Non-college Total %	High School Students %	Employed %	Unemployed %	Housewives %
	Conventional life intolerable	12	10	12	21	8
	Not sure	1	2	2	4	1
c.	Might Prefer to Live in Some Other Country or Society	28	26	26	38	27
5.	**Political Outlook**					
a.	Believe We Are a "Sick" Society	35	32	33	39	41
b.	Own View of Society					
	American way of life is superior to life in other countries	19	24	18	11	19
	There are flaws in our society, but we are flexible enough to solve them	56	52	60	53	55
	System is not flexible; radical change is needed	18	17	15	25	19
	Whole social system should be replaced	7	6	6	10	6
c.	Believe Present System Democratic in Name Only	58	51	61	60	56
d.	Where Real Power Vested					
	Giant corporations	33	23	43	33	28
	Congress	30	35	27	24	31
	President	24	23	24	24	24
	Financiers	16	8	20	20	20
	General public	12	15	10	5	16
	Special interest groups (i.e., labor, religious, etc.)	9	10	10	8	8
	Defense Department	5	4	6	8	4
	CIA	3	2	4	5	3
	Republican Party	3	3	4	3	2
	Democratic Party	2	2	3	3	—

NONCOLLEGE GROUPINGS (Continued)

	Non-college Total %	High School Students %	Em-ployed %	Unem-ployed %	House-wives %
e. *Criticisms of American Society (Agree Strongly or Partially)*					
Business is too concerned with profits and not with public responsibility	92	91	94	92	92
Our foreign policy is based on our own narrow economic and power interests	88	87	89	91	81
People's privacy is being destroyed	84	82	86	83	85
I'm tired of hearing people attack patriotism, morality, and other American values	78	79	77	73	82
There is too much concern with the welfare "bum"	77	78	80	68	74
Basically we are a racist nation	77	75	80	80	74
We are rapidly losing our right to dissent	73	78	71	70	70
There is too much concern with equality and not enough with law and order	71	72	72	71	78
Police should not hesitate to use force to maintain order	69	68	70	63	74
f. *Institutions That Need Fundamental Reform or Elimination*					
Political parties	64	58	67	64	64
Penal system	50	43	53	58	50
Big business	45	37	48	49	47
Military	38	32	42	46	34
High schools	38	38	37	43	31

NONCOLLEGE GROUPINGS (Continued)

	Non-college Total %	High School Students %	Employed %	Unemployed %	House-wives %
Trade unions	34	34	35	36	31
Congress	31	29	31	33	30
FBI	27	21	30	39	28
Mass media	27	27	28	36	23
Supreme Court	24	21	24	32	21
Colleges/universities	21	17	21	29	18
Constitution	13	12	11	20	12

g. *Restraints Willingly and Easily Accepted*

	Non-college Total %	High School Students %	Employed %	Unemployed %	House-wives %
Prohibition against heroin	80	81	80	76	82
Prohibition against mind-expanding drugs	71	72	71	66	78
Power and authority of police	60	62	58	52	69
Power and authority of the "boss" in a work situation	57	56	56	56	65
Prohibition against marijuana	49	51	46	40	62
Settling down to a routine	47	47	43	47	60
Conformity in matters of dress and personal grooming	42	42	40	37	49
Outward conformity for the sake of career or job advancement	37	40	34	34	41
Abiding by laws you do not agree with	24	25	22	20	30

h. *Attention Paid to Minority Groups*

	Non-college Total %	High School Students %	Employed %	Unemployed %	House-wives %
Too much attention	27	25	27	22	34
Too little attention	38	40	37	43	31
Just right amount	27	29	28	22	26
Not sure	8	7	9	14	8

NONCOLLEGE GROUPINGS (Continued)

	Non-college Total %	High School Students %	Em-ployed %	Unem-ployed %	House-wives %
i. *Groups Discriminated Against by Society*					
American Indians	71	70	74	75	65
Homosexuals	66	64	68	69	60
Poor people	64	58	65	71	67
Mexican-Americans	60	58	62	67	56
High school dropouts	60	62	57	69	59
Old people	57	52	62	58	65
Blacks	55	55	54	64	48
Women	37	33	40	42	38
Blue-collar workers	27	23	29	29	25
College students	17	16	19	17	16
j. *Controversial Proposals Favored*					
Cut back defense spending and use the money for domestic needs	75	72	77	78	76
Stricter gun control	63	66	61	58	68
Death penalty for certain crimes	52	53	54	42	57
Legalize marijuana	47	42	52	60	30
Life sentences without parole for drug pushers	45	46	43	39	59
Crack down on pornography in movies, books, etc.	44	46	43	44	49
Grant amnesty for draft evaders	42	41	44	46	36
Limit number of children a family can have	28	29	29	23	25
k. *Reasons Worth Fighting a War for*					
Counteracting aggression	53	48	53	46	54

NONCOLLEGE GROUPINGS (Continued)

	Non-college Total %	High School Students %	Employed %	Unemployed %	Housewives %
Containing communism	50	53	46	45	59
Protecting own national interest	49	51	47	52	51
Protecting our allies	46	48	45	46	42
Fighting for our honor	43	48	40	39	43
Maintaining our position of power in the world	40	43	35	41	46
Keeping a commitment	23	23	20	27	24

Catalog

If you are interested in a list of fine Paperback
books, covering a wide range of subjects
and interests, send your name and address,
requesting your free catalog, to:

McGraw-Hill Paperbacks
1221 Avenue of Americas
New York, N.Y. 10020